States of Mind

States of Mind

ESP and Altered States of Consciousness

Adrian Parker

Taplinger Publishing Company

New York

To Inger

First published in the United States in 1975 by
TAPLINGER PUBLISHING CO., INC.
New York, New York
Copyright © 1975 by Adrian Parker
All rights reserved
Printed in Great Britain

Library of Congress Catalog Card Number: 75-808
ISBN 0-8008-7374-2

Contents

Acknowledgments

The author and publishers are grateful for permission from the following to quote from their publications:

JOURNAL OF THE SOCIETY FOR PSYCHICAL RESEARCH
Barker, J. *Premonitions of the Aberfan Disaster* 1967 (44), pp. 169–180; Beloff, J., and Mandelberg, I. *An attempted validation of the 'Ryzl' technique for training ESP subjects* 1966 (43), pp. 229–49; Edmunds, S., and Jolliffe, D. *A GESP experiment with four hypnotised subjects* 1965 (43), pp. 192–4; Evans, C., and Osborne, E. *An experiment in the electroencephalography of mediumistic trance* 1952 (36), pp. 588–96; Parker, A. *Some success at screening for ESP subjects* 1974 (in press); Stephenson, C. J. *Cambridge ESP-hypnosis* (1958–64) 1965 (43), pp. 77–91; West, D., and Fisk, G. *A dual ESP experiment with clock cards* 1953 (37), pp. 185–97.

AMERICAN ARCHIVES OF GENERAL PSYCHIATRY
GLASS, G. and BOWERS, M. *Chronic psychosis associated with long-term psychotomimetic drug abuse* 1970 (23), pp. 97–130.

GREEN, C. *Lucid Dreams*. Proceedings of the Institute for Psychophysical Research 1968 1 Oxford (b) (published by Hamish Hamilton, London, on behalf of the Institute for Psychophysical Research).

MCCREERY, C. *Physical Phenomena and the Physical World*. Proceedings of the Institute for Psychophysical Research 1973 (4), London (Hamish Hamilton).

6

Author's Preface

In writing this book I am first indebted to those whose research it compiles, and in particular I would like to express my gratitude to Charles Tart of the University of California and Charles Honorton of the Maimonides Medical Center, New York, the two leading authorities in the field to whose work I have made frequent reference.

Special indebtedness is also due to John Beloff of the University of Edinburgh for suggesting the venture and for reading and commenting on the manuscript.

As well as referring to experimental research, I have found it valuable to illustrate extrasensory perception and altered states of consciousness by means of description. For permission to quote in this area I am grateful to the Society for Psychical Research, the American Medical Association, Robert Masters and Jean Housten of the Foundation for Mind Research, and Celia Green and Charles McCreery of the Institute for Psychophysical Research (together with Hamish Hamilton, their publisher).

Thanks are also due to Dr George Glass for his open-mindedness in allowing me to quote one of his case histories in criticism of the medical approach to psychedelics, and to Dr Ronald Shor for his permission to include examples from the Personal Experiences Questionnaire.

I extend thanks to David Bate and other friends who, through discussion, helped me in the formation of ideas.

And, finally, I would like to express appreciation to my parents, and to Bertil and Ulla Wettmark, for providing such a pleasant environment in which to write the book during my tenure of the Perrott-Warwick Studentship in Psychical Research of Trinity College, Cambridge.

Introduction

For a long time experimental psychology, especially in the United States, was so preoccupied with establishing its scientific credentials that it all but lost sight of its proper subject-matter—the nature of mind. Two topics in particular were regarded as beyond the pale: consciousness and the paranormal. The former was rejected because to study it required the use of introspection, and this could never be objective, the latter because it raised again the spectre of the occult from which science had so laboriously extricated itself. But, today, with the passing of the behaviourist era, both these topics are once again attracting the attention of main-stream psychologists. In this book the author makes a bold attempt to bring together these two suspect fields and discusses their relationship to one another. Even ten years ago such a book could not have been published, yet it is a book which, I like to think, would have delighted William James.

Neither the concept of an altered state of consciousness (ASC) nor that of extrasensory perception (ESP) is easy to define and the author wisely refrains from doing so except by way of example. This is because both concepts can only be defined, in the first instance, in negative terms. Roughly, an ASC is any state of mind that differs markedly enough from that which we associate with our normal waking selves. Similarly, any instance in which knowledge is acquired other than via the known sensory channels is, by definition, an instance of ESP or paranormal cognition. But, this having been said, the phenomena that come under each of these headings cover a wide and varied spectrum.

Consider first the range of ASCs. An ASC may be something quite commonplace, like a nocturnal dream, or it may be something bizarre and uncanny, like a mediumistic trance, a state of possession, a secondary personality. Again, it may be something morbid or terrifying, like a delirium or a psychotic episode, or else something sublime or ecstatic, like the visions of a mystic. Finally it may come about suddenly of its own accord, like an out-of-body experience or a waking hallucination, or it may have to be deliberately induced by means of drugs, hypnosis or techniques of meditation. At the very end of this book the author attempts to tabulate the varieties of ASC both in terms of their phenomenology, the kind of world that is perceived in such a state, and in terms of the nature of the self that is involved as the subject of the experience. But, as he points out, in practice one such experience slides very easily into another; it is only a step from the pathological to the mystical or from a state of depersonalisation to a full-blown out-of-body experience. Which direction it takes may depend very much on the social context, whether it be clinical or religious or whether the subject finds himself in a supportive setting or not.

Of special interest in this connection is Chapter Seven on 'Psychedelic States'. The author is right, I think, in tracing the present vogue for ASCs to the so-called 'psychedelic revolution' of the early 1960s. Whether this revolution was a benign one, as the author believes, is perhaps a matter of controversy. Since that time society has found itself saddled with a vast drug problem which it is still seeking to control and contain. It is no longer so easy for us to share the blithe enthusiasm for the mind-liberating, mind-expanding potentialities of drugs expressed so eloquently by the late Aldous Huxley, the rightful inaugurator of the psychedelic revolution. Nevertheless, the author, speaking no doubt for his generation, takes a firm and positive stand on this issue. In particular, he deplores the fact that, owing to what he regards as the panic reaction of the authorities, it has now become virtually impossible to do any systematic psychological research on the psychedelic drugs.

9

But if it required a revolution to bring home to us the richness and diversity of consciousness, it was thanks to the methodology and instrumentation developed in the behaviourist laboratory that this revival of interest in introspective psychology could be taken so much further than was possible in the days of William James. Thus the whole area of sleep research was transformed by the new possibilities of monitoring the subject's brain activities during sleep by the use of the electroencephalogram (EEG) apparatus. For it was now possible to wake the dreamer at the precise point when he was emerging from his dream phase and we no longer needed to base our knowledge of dreams, those most private of inner experiences, on what the subject could remember of them the following day.

Another no less striking example of the application of objective techniques to subjective states comes from the sphere of meditation. In Chapter Eight, the author reports on the findings of certain Indian physiologists on the physiological concomitants of Yoga, and on the findings of Japanese workers on the physiological effects of Zen meditation. The introduction of biofeedback techniques, moreover, has made it possible for the ordinary subject to acquire something of the same control over his bodily functions as the practitioners of these Eastern disciplines. Even rats, apparently, can now be conditioned to control bodily and visceral processes including blood-pressure, using the self-stimulation of their pleasure-centres as the reinforcement. At the same time there are important differences in the overall physiological pattern produced in man by means of biofeedback conditioning techniques and those brought about by the practice of meditation. Nevertheless, where biofeedback can be used to give the subject control over his brain activity, in particular over the incidence of alpha-rhythm in his EEG output, something resembling a state of meditation or trance can be sustained.

Nor is it only with respect to measurement and the application of objective methods that we are the beneficiaries of behaviourist psychology. In matters of experimental design, especially where this concerns the contaminating effects of uncontrolled artifacts, including experimenter-effects, we have learnt many salutary lessons and have become vastly more sophisticated. Thus the author speaks of experiments using double or even triple blind experimental designs to insure against the invalidating consequences of expectancy effects. The long drawn-out controversy which the author discusses in Chapter Two, between those of the Tart-Hilgard school who regard hypnosis as a genuine ASC, and those of the Barber-Calverley-Sarbin school who regard hypnosis as nothing more than just a special kind of role-playing, reflects well this new sophistication, though I think the author is justified, in the end, in siding with the former position.

Let us turn now to the question of ESP. As the author rightly points out in his first chapter, parapsychology during the behaviourist era took on a protective colouring. Its pre-occupation with the aseptic approach of card-guessing has left a widespread impression that ESP may be identified with the small statistical bias that constitutes the outcome of a successful ESP experiment. Thus, even the eminent philosopher A. J. Ayer could say recently about ESP that: 'it is no more than a colourful way of summarizing a mildly interesting collection of statistics'.[1]

Statistical artifact or second sight? I hope that this book, if it does nothing more, will help to dispel the idea of ESP as a minor anomaly of people's guessing behaviour and encourage us to think of it as perhaps one of the cardinal properties of mind. For the author follows its manifold ramifications in history and in its naturalistic setting. We watch it emerging from the early demonstrations of the mesmerists, from the practices of spiritualism and mediumship and as it shows itself in spontaneous out-of-body or out-of-time experiences, or in premonitory dreams. Of course, in every instance where the authenticity of the phenomenon can be challenged, the evidence is always less than fully satisfactory—otherwise the existence of ESP would no longer be controversial—but it would be an entirely un-

[1] *The Listener*, 20th September 1973, p. 375.

warranted curtailment of the concept to ignore this rich mine of qualitative evidence and restrict our gaze to quantitative guessing-tests.

What conclusions can we draw from this book about the relationship between ESP and ASCs? It must be admitted that so far as our present understanding goes the relationship is complex, devious and still rather tenuous. No one has yet discovered an ASC which automatically produces ESP. If, for example, the new pharmacopoeia available to the psycho-pharmacologist contained even one drug that conferred tele-pathic or clairvoyant powers, parapsychology would now be a very different science. ESP experiences have been reported in connection with drug-induced states or with states of medita-tion, as the author mentions, but they have been largely of an anecdotal and sporadic kind. Of all the relationships the author deals with, that between ESP and hypnosis has probably received the most attention, going back as it does to the early days of the mesmerist movement. But, while some undoubtedly dramatic results have been reported with subjects in a deep hypnotic trance, no definite proof has yet emerged that hypnosis enhances ESP. Hopes rose again during the 1960s when news came from Prague that a certain Dr Ryzl was using hypnosis to train subjects to develop their ESP abilities. But not only have other parapsychologists been unable to confirm his claims; Ryzl himself, who now works in the United States, has failed to provide any convincing confirmation of them either. Meanwhile, his one star subject, Pavel Stepanek, who has been internationally investigated, does his guessing in the ordinary waking state.

The most important work to come out of the new rapproche-ment between parapsychology and introspective psychology is, in my opinion, the experiments conducted by the team attached to the Maimonides Hospital in Brooklyn, New York. The author describes their researches in Chapter Four in his section on the 'Parapsychology of Dreams'. Basically, these were attempts to demonstrate a telepathic influence on a subject's dream-imagery. An authoritative yet popular account of the work of the Maimonides Dream Laboratory during its ten years of existence can be found in the book by M. Ullman, S. Krippner and A. Vaughan entitled *Dream Telepathy* (Turnstone Books. London, 1973). Although their work is of prime importance as an example of a systematic attack on a parapsychological problem which has helped to enlarge the scope of parapsychology, its statistical significance is, as so often happens, marginal and confined to a few successful subjects. As the author remarks at the end of Chapter Four, the real puzzle is that there should be any effect at all when using highly artificial target material such as reproductions of art. It is also odd that the selected target should produce any effect on a sleeping subject when all around him other people may be looking at objects and pictures that presumably exert no influence at all. It seems, therefore, that the author is right when he suggests that it is the experimental situation that counts, that if both experimenter and subject are highly motivated in the ESP task then the 'demand characteristics' of that task operate so as to force the dream consciousness to attend to the ESP targets in a way which he compares to the operation of a post-hypnotic suggestion.

At the present time much interest is centred on the possibility that what does enhance ESP is not so much some specific ASC but the transition that occurs when a subject shifts from one ASC to another, especially from an outward-oriented state to an inner-directed state. The author pays particular attention to this hypothesis which he discusses in Chapter One and again in Chapter Eight in his section on 'Biofeedback, Alpha States and ESP' and he reverts to it at the end of the book in Chapter Nine. But all the relevant work in this connection is of such recent origin and the results still so precarious that it would be rash to regard this as more than a pointer to further research.

I began by pointing out that the repudiation of behaviourism has opened up whole new vistas to the psychologist that invite exploration. To this we may add that it has also allowed us to take a more positive, more helpful and more rounded view of man and his position in the scheme of things. Theories of motivation are no longer constrained to treat the organism as a homeostat activated only by the impulse to restore an initial state of equilibrium. Theories of personality need no longer treat the individual as a mere battleground for conflicting urges and desires as in the classic Freudian formulation. Curiosity and creativity have come to be recognised as features of human behaviour no less than our biological drives; self-fulfilment and self-transcendence can be goals of human endeavour no less than self-preservation and self-assertion. In such a context the kinds of states with which this book deals become relevant and important.

But we must exercise restraint if we are not to sacrifice the hard-won intellectual gains of previous, more austere approaches. We do not yet know how far we can go while remaining within the ambit of science. Eastern philosophies afford a ready-made conceptual framework of great subtlety and richness within which both the varieties of consciousness and of paranormal phenomena can make some kind of sense. Certainly it is not easy for Western science to make sense of a universe where psychological-type laws seem to prevail over physical ones. And yet, those of us who have been brought up in Western modes of thought cannot easily embrace an alien metaphysics stemming from an entirely different tradition, and nor can we readily reconcile the two. Western science, we must not forget, has stood us in good stead now for some centuries during which time human knowledge has grown as never before. It remains to be seen how successfully it can cope with this new challenge.

JOHN BELOFF

1
ESP and Consciousness

Probably more than at any other time in history, there is today a preoccupation with personal relationships, subjective reality and inner experience. We are discovering that as well as an external world, we have access to internal realities—states of mind which transcend our waking consciousness and can provide a rich source of meaningful experience and potential. These are the altered states of consciousness (ASCs) we know as dream states, trance states, psychedelic experiences and meditation, which can give a new perspective to our relationship with the world around, a perspective which may sometimes include knowledge derived by extrasensory perception (ESP). While this may not of itself be new (because psychic phenomena have traditionally and historically been associated with trances and mystic states) it is something which has only recently been confirmed by scientific methods. This book comes then as a progress report on the exploration of this inner reality, but to understand why this exploration took so long, we need to say something about the context in which this research developed.

Parapsychology, the scientific study of psychic phenomena, grew out of the Victorian search for proof of an after life by investigation of ghosts and mediums. During the 1930s and '40s, it underwent a scientific transformation when it became concerned with ESP card guessing tests and experiments. This was akin to the way in which psychology had achieved respectability by its use of rats for experiments on learning and perception. ESP cards provided parapsychology with a similar objective approach.

The technique required that an individual guess the content of cards that could be seen by others, and success was evaluated statistically by comparison with what could be expected by chance. But both sciences became victims of their methodologies, so that in psychology it became fashionable to talk only of 'behavioural variables' and in parapsychology, ESP scores were referred to as 'deviations for chance expectancy'. The mention of consciousness and subjective experience became taboo and unscientific, while ASCs were shunted across to psychiatry—to be diagnosed usually as psychotic states. No doubt part of this was due to the emphasis on logic and intellectualism integral to Western science in which, of course, subjective reality has no part. Even the therapeutically orientated psychoanalysts regarded feelings as a threat to ego control and saw the person as a battleground for dark unconscious forces.

By contrast, subjective reality and ASCs are revered in most other cultures. Charles Tart in the editorial to his excellent collection of articles on altered states (1972) writes: 'Many primitive peoples . . . believe that almost every normal adult has the ability to go into a trance state and be possessed by a god; the adult who cannot do this is a psychological cripple.' In the field of psychology at present, the situation is changing with the emergence of humanistic and existential approaches where experiencing and awareness are given priority. For a long time parapsychology made no advance because of its attempt to apply the cause and effect concepts of physics to phenomena that seemed to contradict logic itself. It now seems likely that parapsychology will find its long-awaited conceptual and theoretical basis in ASCs which, at the same time, may provide a point where parapsychology can integrate with psychology rather than remaining, as it has done, a problem child.

Nearly all of these changes have occurred in the last decade and, since we cannot write off the other eighty years of history in a few lines, something must be said about how the situation arose where consciousness through the use of its intellect almost succeeded in eliminating itself as a useful concept.

Psychology and consciousness

During this century behaviourism and psychoanalysis have been the two main trends in psychology. Behaviourism—with its philosophy of excluding all reference to subjective experience and its emphasis on stimulus and response—on objective aspects of behaviour left psychology in such a position that the late Sir Cyril Burt (1962) satirised: 'Psychology having first bargained away its soul and then gone out of its mind, seems now, as it faces an untimely end, to have lost all consciousness.' Another-well known psychologist, Ernest Hilgard (1969), explained the reason for this: 'Psychologists are trying to be scientists like other scientists and they will do anything to be proper about it even to the point of denying some of their subject matter.' Thus, in order to be scientific and to control and predict behaviour in terms of variables, references to consciousness and states of mind that were not observable had to be left out.

Psychoanalysis, the other major trend, was equally mechanistic in describing the human organism in terms of static and dynamic entities derived from the physics of the period in which Freud was educated. Thus, a person was viewed as a set of complexes and unconscious forces with the ego as the controlling centre. When it came to therapy, a fundamental contradiction was always apparent; repression of the instincts was considered necessary for adjustment to society, yet expression of instincts was necessary for self-fulfilment and health. The mistake lay in the assumption that defences are necessary for psychological adjustment, that a person without defences would be an uncontrollable psychopath. Another fallacy common to both behaviourism and psychoanalysis was the application of the cause and effect model (from physics) to thought and action. It is difficult to see what cause and effect imply when we talk about 'the unity of thought', and it can be argued that it is preferable to talk of meaningful relations between aspects of experience (Rycroft 1966).

Recently, a third approach to human experience has gained

support. We mentioned before the existential or phenomenological orientation in which theories and concepts peculiar to
experiencing are used but phrased in terms amenable to
research and experimentation. This has proved so successful
that psychology has seen a revival of experiencing and
consciousness. (See, for example, Rogers 1961, Beloff 1962,
Holt 1964, Bannister 1968, Warr 1973.) We shall look next at
how a parallel set of changes has influenced the development
of ideas in parapsychology.

Parapsychology and consciousness

The scientific study of the paranormal, or psychical research
as it was then known, began in the late nineteenth century with
the formation of the Society for Psychical Research. Many
distinguished philosophers and scientists were among the early
members. The main motivation for psychical research then was
the survival problem: whether or not there was life after
bodily death. In the age of Victorian science the main source of
evidence for the non-physical nature of the mind lay in the
claims of spiritualism. By applying the methods of science to
this problem, the early investigators expected to have an answer
within a generation.

Consequently, most of the early research was concerned
with collecting records of spontaneous cases of apparitions,
investigations of mediums, and experiments on telepathy and
hypnosis. However, the major advance was to come in 1927
with the establishment of a Parapsychology Laboratory at
Duke University by the distinguished psychologist William
McDougall. McDougall appointed as its director an articulate
and enthusiastic researcher, J. B. Rhine, and it was Rhine who
gave parapsychology its terminology and devised the first
standardised, objective guessing tests of ESP. Using these,
Rhine discovered that many subjects could identify cards at a
much higher rate than could be accounted for by the laws of
chance. He distinguished three major forms of ESP as telepathy
(the awareness of another individual's thoughts), clairvoyance
(the awareness of events or objects), and precognition (the

prophetic knowledge of events). All were achieved by means other than the known senses. Rhine also produced evidence for psychokinesis—the influence of thoughts on the movement of objects. Collectively, psychic phenomena are termed psi or paranormal occurrences.

Despite the objective nature of the evidence, ESP became the subject of heated, often prejudiced debate in the scientific world. Forty years later the controversy is still raging, but as more and more evidence appears, the sceptics are harder pressed to support their case. It is unfortunate that critics usually refer to thirty-year-old experiments rather than concerning themselves with contemporary evidence. One high-scoring subject—Pavel Stepanek—produced good results with at least a dozen different experimenters (all of whom recorded favourable opinions) during his study by Gaither Pratt at the University of Virginia (1973).

Consequently, attitudes towards ESP seem to be softening. Orthodox scientific journals now occasionally publish research, and the Parapsychology Association—an international body of research workers—was admitted to the American Association for the Advancement of Science in 1969. Much publicity was also gained by the partially successful ESP experiment during the Apollo 14 mission (Mitchell 1971).

Having said this, it must be admitted that there are still problems that prevent parapsychology from obtaining the full backing it needs. One is the lack of a theoretical framework in which to fit the findings but, as was suggested, this seems likely to be developed, and one of the arguments put forward later will be that ASCs can provide this context. The other problem is that of the replication or 'reproducibility' of findings, which is a more serious one (Beloff 1967). In other words, the conditions necessary for the detection or development of ESP abilities in individuals have so far proved impossible to specify with any degree of confidence, which means we can say that ESP exists but that very little is known about it.

Much of the research followed the same pattern as psychology experiments, attempting to isolate discrete behavioural · variables or personality traits which could then be controlled and manipulated with some precision. Although major research has been done into personality characteristics of ESP scorers for over thirty years, attempts to repeat specific findings have largely failed. Part of the problem arose because of a conflict between stagnation and alienation; was it better to stay within established frameworks in an attempt to develop theories which reconciled ESP with physics—and risk stagnation if this failed? Or was it better to attempt to develop new and radical approaches at the risk of further alienation? Almost totally, the former view prevailed and, until recently, attempts to find a repeatable experiment had also failed, and wave theories of telepathy proved inapplicable because ESP seems to have no definite relationship to distance, time or even target factors (Rao 1966).

Psychology ran into a similar paradoxical problem by trying to apply inadequate scientific methods based on the nineteenth-century physical sciences.

Ironically, one of the main influences on ESP seems to be the interpersonal conditions of the experiment—the relationship between subject and experimenter, and the subject's motivation and interest in the task. Experimenters themselves may have particular influence on their own results, and one way of circumventing this problem has been to use animals as experimental subjects to try and eliminate the interpersonal factor. Precognition experiments have been used to avoid giving cues to which the animal may respond. The technique is a simple one which allows the animal to make a choice where one decision will have a desirable outcome and the other an undesirable outcome. For example, if the animal is in one part of a cage it may receive a minor shock while in another it avoids it. The sequence of the contingency is random so we can see whether it does better than it would by chance. Whether this technique, or modifications of it (Parker 1974), will provide the long sought-after, repeatable ESP experiment is unknown, but it seems probable that the lack of repeatability in most ESP experiments could be due to neglecting to take account of the influence of interpersonal subtleties. But if parapsychology has neglected to study these factors, an even larger omission concerns knowledge of the state of consciousness of ESP subjects during their best performances.

Subjective state and interpersonal factors

The main factors relating to ESP may well be the subjective state of the individual together with interpersonal factors such as expectancy, the social situation, and the individual's relationship to the others involved in the experiment.

Unfortunately, the behaviouristic Zeitgeist (bias) penetrated parapsychology to the extent that until very recently there was a complete absence of any assessment of the states of consciousness of subjects during their ESP tests. Charles Honorton, one of the younger professional parapsychologists, has commented on this:

In view of the behaviouristic Zeitgeist it is perhaps not surprising that early proponents of the card guessing paradigm . . . largely disregarded their subjects' internal states and focused instead on relatively gross behavioural criteria. (Honorton 1973.)

However, in an important survey and reanalysis of the old experimental work with high-scoring ESP subjects, Rhea White (1964) produced evidence (contrary to the accepted view) that many of these subjects were in fact in what could be called ASCs. She was even able to quote Rhine as saying: 'Several subjects have described their ESP experiences as involving a state of "detachment", "abstraction", "relaxation" and the like.' Moreover, Rhine often used the word 'trance' to describe the appearance of many of his high-scoring ESP subjects. In surveying the remainder of the literature which describes the ESP subject's state of awareness during testing, Rhea White concludes that they implicate a state of passivity in which tension builds up, rather like the effort involved in recalling a forgotten name. But she thinks this may be more than just relaxation, and may indicate 'another level of the self, one seldom tapped in the general run of parapsychological experiments to which the word "guess" can no longer be applied'. Further confirmation of the existence of a relationship between success at ESP tests and states of awareness comes in the description of his own state of mind by a recently discovered high-scoring subject. The experimenters (Kelly and Kanthamani 1972) note how he describes his state as '"de-egoisation", by which he means putting himself in a state of intense, alert passivity, waiting for the information to present itself, whatever it may be, relative to his desires or expectations'. As we shall see in the next chapter, there exists a small percentage of the population who are susceptible to spontaneous trance states or hypnosis-type experiences (Tart and Hilgard 1966, Shor *et al.* 1962) who may constitute the sample in which ESP subjects are found.

The other major consideration relating to ESP, interpersonal influences, concerns such effects as the subject's expectancies and his relationship with the experimenter. These may be important determinants of the outcome of the ordinary psychology experiment (Orne 1959, Rosenthal 1966), and although there is a dearth of parapsychological experimentation in this area, such research as there is suggests that the relationship between subject and experimenter may be even more critical here (Pratt and Price 1938).

Precisely how these effects operate is unknown; recently (Honorton 1972c) it has been found that such apparently superficial behaviour as whether or not experimenters smiled and greeted their subjects casually had a significant effect on scores. The effect probably goes much deeper than this, and there is an interesting experiment carried out by Donald West and the late G. W. Fisk (1953) which suggests that the experimenter need not be actually present to affect his results. They found their subjects only produced significantly high scores on the cards sealed by Fisk while the scores on West's cards did not differ from chance expectancy. This occurred despite the fact that they had not been informed of West's participation, and suggests that a paranormal factor could be involved.

Other important considerations are undoubtedly motivation and empathy. Indeed, it now seems likely that Rhine's extraordinary success during the 1930s can be partly attributed to his ability to motivate subjects (Rhine 1964). Expectancy of success is probably part of this, and it has been shown many times that those who have this expectancy and believe in ESP score significantly higher than disbelievers (Palmer 1971). As for empathy, research tends to confirm the popular view that ESP occurs more often in close, intimate relationships (Stuart 1946, Rice and Townsend 1964).

As well as affecting the manifestation of ESP experiences, interpersonal influences also appear to affect experiences during ASCs. For example, subjects taking part in dream research will usually find that the content of their dreams on the first night deals largely with the fact that they are the subject of experiment. In an attempt to explain hypnosis, Theodore Barber has suggested that all the experiences we normally attribute to the existence of a trance state can be explained entirely by interpersonal factors, and there is no need to use the word trance at all. Undoubtedly, psychedelic states are among the most susceptible to the effects of expectancy and situation. The depth and type of experience depend substantially on the amount of preparation and support the individual is given. In fact, expectancy concerning a particular ASC seems to determine whether that experience is an enhancing or a disturbing one, and many experiences which were previously regarded as pathological can be better understood in these terms.

All of this implies that there is a complex but critically important interaction between subjective state, interpersonal effects and extrasensory perception. Some of this we will attempt to unravel in future chapters, but it remains to be discussed as to why these experiences are important and what they mean.

The implications of ESP and ASCs
The importance of ASCs becomes obvious when we consider how much of our existence they account for. Making allow-

ances for the time spent in dream states, fantasy and reverie periods, the amount of time spent in our logical rational state (the one we usually identify with consciousness), is quite small. Moreover, since the advent of the EEG (electroencephalograph) machine to record brain electrical activity, and the EOG (electro-oculograph) to measure eye movements which are indices of dreaming, it seems probable that there is no period of complete absence of consciousness or awareness, except perhaps in a coma or in death. Using these machines, it has been shown that there are other types of awareness during sleep besides dreaming. Dreams tend to occur in periods of REM (rapid eye movement) activity, but 'thought dreams' can occur in non-REM periods, which account for the remaining part of sleep. These are periods of thinking rather than hallucinatory imagery. As well as this, the period between waking and sleeping has recently been shown to involve at least three different 'ego states' or levels of intactness of the self. There also appear to be other less common but distinct dream states such as the 'lucid dream' where the subject is aware that he is dreaming and is able to some extent to control the dream content. These are just the states of consciousness associated with sleep, but there are many other states of awareness. The great American psychologist William James, partly as a result of his experiences with nitrous oxide, concluded:

Our normal waking consciousness . . . is but one special state of consciousness, whilst all about it, parted from it by the filmiest of screens, there lie potential forms of consciousness entirely different. We may go through life without suspecting their existence; but apply the requisite stimulus, and at a touch they are there in all their completeness. . . . No account of the universe in its totality can be final which leaves these other forms of consciousness quite disregarded. (James 1901.)

But what makes ASCs more than bizarre oddities of nature is their association with ESP and their therapeutic and creative potential.

ESP has importance at several levels. It has philosophical and religious implications with regard to the relation of the mind to the brain in suggesting that consciousness, or at least perception, can transcend the parameters of the brain. 'Parapsychology is the ultimate battleground upon which theories of the mind-body relationship will be fought' (John Beloff 1962). Eventually, we may be forced to the viewpoint that mental events have their own 'psycho-space' in terms of our emotional proximity or remoteness from each other's experiences. At the very least, ESP suggests that the barriers between us are not as great as we usually conceive. And in some aspects of the association of ESP with ASCs seems to give support to the claims of some of those states for unity of consciousness with the world. Mystical and meditation states, for example, are often claimed to attain a transcendental level in which a direct perception or unity with reality is reached. Whether or not this is true, it is consistent with the view of the great German philosopher Emmanuel Kant who argued that, in order to answer such questions as the ultimate nature of reality, we would have to transcend the very intellect that posed them, which is in fact what has been claimed in some ASCs. These are obviously knotty problems which will have to be looked at in more detail later. But whatever the status of these 'other realities' associated with ESP and ASCs, they do have subjective validity and meaning for the individual, an essential part of which is the self-exploration they seem to entail when a more expansive and deeper level of the self may be perceived. It is from this they derive their creative and therapeutic potential.

Psychologists often talk of two modes or poles of thought, the realistic and the imaginative. There is much evidence that the realistic, logical mode is associated with the acquisition of information while creative inspiration comes during ASCs, often hypogogic, fantasy, or dream states. The writings of many well-known artists and scientists illustrate this point (Ghiselin 1952), a noted example being Kekulé's discovery of the formula for the benzene ring (a configuration of the carbon and hydrogen atoms in the formula for benzene), represented during a dream by twirling snakes. Mozart also wrote that his ideas came during sleepless nights, but 'whence and how they came I know not'. Likewise, Henri Poincaré for fifteen days tried to derive a certain mathematical function until at last, during a sleepless night, 'ideas arose in crowds, I felt them collide until pairs locked'. He concluded, 'Is not the subliminal self superior to the conscious self?'

Mystical experiences have also given rise to scientific and artistic creations, the works of Johannes Kepler and William Blake being examples of this. And psychedelic drugs have for some time been the subject of controversy as to whether they facilitate creativity. While many subjective reports claim that they do, too little research has been done in this area to permit a definite conclusion. There is tentative evidence that when preparation is adequate and the situation conducive, they may have enormous creative potential.

The question that emerges from this asks from whence derives the information? Is it from a Freudian unconscious of un-resolved feelings and experiences, or does this information point to a more transcendental or transpersonal level such as envisaged by Jung? One class of experiences which seem to link creativity and the paranormal support the latter interpreta-tion. These are the pseudo-reincarnation cases, cases of secondary personality. The most mysterious is that reported by Walter Franklin Prince of the American Society for Psychical Research (1927) involving Mrs Curran, a housewife who was entertaining herself and a friend with automatic writing using a ouija board when it wrote: 'Many moons ago I lived. Again I come. Patience Worth my name.' Patience Worth claimed she was born in England in the seventeenth century, and later emigrated to America where she was killed by Indians. She produced descriptions of her life but could give no evidence, insisting only that her utterances were of value. Her grammar, vocabulary and phrases were often close to her period and seemed far beyond the capabilities of Mrs Curran's formal education—which was very little. She had never been out of the Mid West, had never seen the sea, and had a limited knowledge

of literature. Even if she had attempted to acquire the specialised knowledge, it would still have been a feat, and she dictated
at a rate that was sometimes too fast for most stenographers.
Five books and 500 lengthy poems were dictated, some of which
won prizes and literary acclaim. Her story of the time of
Christ, 'The Sorry Tale', was applauded by many newspaper
reviewers who were unaware of its occult origins. In one way
'Patience' outdid herself; her phrases and grammar were not
just appropriate to the seventeenth century but were sometimes
a pastiche of many periods and dialects. They varied from 90
per cent Anglo Saxon to a nineteenth-century style and contained many foreign and obsolete words. She displayed much
historical and geographical knowledge, all of which seemed to
transcend Mrs Curran's normal abilities, and produced epigrams
and had a sense of humour. What was also impressive was that
she could dictate aphorisms on any suggested topic without
corrections, at a speed which many writers of the time, such as
Walt Whitman, thought impossible. At that time, attempts to
explain the case included references to 'dissociations' and 'subliminal selves', as well as the usual spirit hypothesis. But often
these served only to hide ignorance. Some cases of multiple
personality, common during the late nineteenth century,
would be understood now in psychodynamic or Jungian terms
as an expression of repressed or opposite parts of the dominant
personality, but the Patience Worth case seems to involve
more than this.

For whatever reason, such cases are rare today, but one
recently publicised is that of Rosemary Brown. Again, an
ordinary housewife with apparently no more than an elemen-
tary education in music, she produced music which she claimed
was dictated to her by many of the great composers. Her list of
compositions were attributed to many famous musicians
including Beethoven, Bach, Brahms, Chopin, Debussy, Liszt,
Schubert and Rakhmaninov. Most authorities agree that the
music is of their style, and that the compositions are not com-
mensurate with Rosemary Brown's formal musical education.
But they also agree that they are improvisations and reworkings

rather than new creations. Although this is not precisely a 'reincarnation' or a secondary personality type of case, it may involve similar dramatisations.

One fairly obvious implication of these cases is that they raise the question of a reappraisal of traditional notions of the unconscious. Rather than regard the unconscious as a sinister refuge for the dark satanic forces of the mind, a more positive approach may imply that the unconscious is not an entity but represents potential forms of experience, some of which may have a far greater creative level than the waking state.

Despite the fact that ASCs in Western culture have usually been regarded as pathological, there is an impressive amount of research to indicate that they may also be therapeutically meaningful, given the right context. Dreams, for example, are normally discounted in the West as being an unpleasant interruption to our waking life, but there are societies which have attributed great importance to them. The Senoi, a Malaysian tribe, seem to regard the line between waking and dreaming life as blurred and indistinct. They practise a form of group therapy and dream analysis similar to methods used by modern encounter groups. A distinctive and possibly related feature of the Senoi is that they have had no record of violent crime or warfare for several hundred years (Stewart 1966). At a more experimental level, there is evidence that the recall of dreams is associated with a less defensive and more secure personality structure (Foulkes 1966). Research on psychedelic effects has also shown that, rather than being of necessity a psychotic-type experience, if properly prepared to give the right support, it can promote psychological growth among both the normal population and some of those suffering from any of a wide range of psychiatric disorders (e.g. Masters and Housten 1966, Mogar and Savage 1964).

Mystical experiences may also be therapeutically meaningful. The existential psychologist Abraham Maslow has described the importance of what he calls 'peak experiences' for psychological health. These are oceanic, mystical or cosmic-type experiences in which the world is perceived with enhanced meaning. In support of this, Maslow quotes peak experiences occurring in many people who are or were generally regarded as self-fulfilled individuals, such as Abraham Lincoln, Walt Whitman and William James (Maslow 1962). Another related area which is gaining prominence is that of encounter groups and groups involving the human potential movement generally. Stemming from such diverse therapies as those of William Reich, Carl Rogers and Frederick Perls, the underlying principle is to explore more authentic ways of relating to others by exposing social games and using non-verbal and other forms of personal communication. The attempt is to create at the same time a warm, accepting atmosphere in which repressed aspects of the self can be explored. The resulting experience is intended to be therapeutic in expanding awareness, lowering defensiveness and increasing sensitivity.

Accompanying these various explorations and expansions of consciousness are frequent reports of paranormal phenomena, so again comes the implication that these experiences involve more than a fantasy reality. We will look next at the evidence for this, which will form a major part of the network of the book, and then consider the suggestion that in order to understand the relation of ESP to ASC we may need to use the approach we mentioned earlier—that of the phenomenological analysis of attributing validity to what subjects actually experience.

PSI and states of consciousness

At an anecdotal level, there is an enormous literature on psi (i.e. paranormal experiences) associated with unusual states of consciousness, and at an experimental level an impressive case can also be made for a link between paranormal events—ESP in particular—and ASCs. In terms of the number of reported studies alone the evidence is impressive. In research on hypnosis, nine out of twelve studies comparing ESP performance in the waking state to ESP performance in the hypnotic state produced significant differences. In dream research, nine out of twelve projects produced significant findings indicative of ESP, and in research on alpha relaxation states there have been now about thirteen studies which suggest there is a relationship between the subjective state accompanied by alpha rhythm and ESP. In others, such as the psychedelic state and out-of-the-body experiences, the number of projects have been much fewer but results also favour an association with ESP. Where there are discrepancies in findings, they seem easily explicable in terms of the interpersonal variables we mentioned earlier.

A lot of the credit for the research in this area must go to the Maimonides Dream Laboratory in New York where most (but not all) of the research has been carried out. They have been especially innovative in the designs they have used to try and find the closest approximation to real life telepathic and extrasensory phenomena. To simulate emotional experiences in their dream research, they used postcard reproductions of paintings as ESP targets on which the sender or 'agent' for the experience concentrated, and 'sensory bombardment' where the agent was subjected to emotional stimuli in an audio-visual chamber. A recent study even used audience participation at a concert given by the pop group *The Grateful Dead* in order to enhance the emotional effect. But in all of these techniques careful, objective (statistical) methods of evaluating the results were used.

Perhaps the greatest achievement of all this research was a political one. A decade ago parapsychology was financed and carried out almost entirely on an amateur basis, but with the focusing of research on ASCs, distinguished psychologists such as Charles Tart, David Foulkes, Joe Kamiya, Jean Housten and R. E. L. Masters have also given their support to parapsychology, and this collaboration has gone a long way towards helping the integration of the two sciences.

On the other hand, new phenomena often need completely new approaches and both ASCs and ESP may not be meaningfully translated into the language of behavioural variables—which, as we remarked earlier, is based on an outdated physics model.

Charles Tart, who is probably the most authoritative figure in this area of research, has come to a similar conclusion:

We must develop some new theoretical structures out of the observational material of our field instead of borrowing from other areas. . . . We do not yet have meaningful enough approaches to study either psi or altered states of consciousness. (Tart 1970.)

In an important publication in the orthodox magazine *Science*—which must herald a radical change of attitude to research in this area—Tart (1972) proposed that some of these new theoretical structures lay in the development of what he called 'state specific sciences'. By this he meant that in order to understand the phenomena of an ASC the scientist-observer must be in the particular state he is trying to interpret. In other words, it is of no value when a subject in a mystical state reports an experience of unity with the universe if the scientist regards it as a psychotic symptom. Instead, to evaluate it, the scientist must experience the state himself. However, what distinguishes the 'state specific science' from religion is the 'commitment of the scientist to re-examine his own belief system'—and to make predictions and generalisations about such experiences which can be later tested. Each state then has its own validity and its own reality although there may be some common perspective where they overlap. Similar views have been advanced by other scientists working in this area. Willis Harman, distinguished for his research on psychedelic experiences, writes: 'For the present it appears that one and the same model is not appropriate for ordering both man's experiences with the physical world and the experiences with his inner life.' (Quoted in Blewett 1963.) Ramakrishna Rao, an Indian parapsychologist who trained at Duke University, found that while his training made him 'obsessed with manipulating variables and obtaining results', in order to understand the phenomena he had to return to the traditional approaches of the East which he had previously abandoned (Rao 1973).

The orientation which seems consistent with all these views

is the phenomenological one. This is an existential and empirical approach in which subjective experiences are accepted as real and meaningful but analysed to reveal common features and relationships. The phenomenological method has been used profitably to give an understanding of the ramifications of psychedelic experiences (Masters and Housten 1966) and mediumship (Broad 1962). One specific method which has proved extremely useful is the simple procedure of requiring subjects to produce a 'state report', to name the level of consciousness they have reached, on a scale, during various stages of the experiment. Using this, it has been found that particular state reports are associated with a specific range of phenomena and experiences. (See, for example, Tart 1972c for the use of these scales in hypnosis, and for the application of similar scales to hypnotic dreams, Tart 1966. For the application of scales to alpha states see Honorton *et al.* 1971, and to sensory deprivation states, Honorton *et al.* 1973.)

One practical result of this is that parapsychology now has its first experimentally-derived functional hypothesis. This hypothesis is that ESP emerges during a change or movement in the state of consciousness.

The change in state hypothesis
Although the hypothesis is largely empirically derived, it was first advanced by the eminent psychologist (and parapsychologist), Gardner Murphy. In 1966, comparing ESP and creativity, he concluded that ESP may involve 'a rapid *movement*, say, from a relaxed to a highly active state, or from a highly integrated to a very dissociated state.' The most recent and formal statement of the hypothesis has been by Charles Honorton (1973): 'Relatively large and rapid shifts in state will be associated with enhanced ESP performance.' The evidence in support of it comes from research on hypnotic dreams, the alpha relaxation state and sensory deprivation experiences in which state reports were studied in relation to ESP scores. In the three studies, Honorton and co-workers (Honorton 1972, Honorton *et al.* 1971, Honorton *et al.* 1972) found the greatest ESP

scores were associated with a change in state. The available evidence also suggests that the critical change is a shift to an internal subjective state. But why should this be, why should ESP occur during a shift towards subjective realities?

'Inner space' and ESP

If, as we suggested previously, interpersonal factors are as crucial to the emergence of ESP as the evidence seems to suggest, then we may be justified in talking of an inner or psychological space which links individuals according to their emotional and empathic proximity. Consequently, telepathy may occur as an overlap in our inner worlds determined by the closeness of our experiences, associations and emotions. Clairvoyance may similarly depend on emotional or meaningful association with the place or object. If we assume this—and it is a vast assumption—it helps to resolve one of the great problems in parapsychology, the independence of distance and the selectivity of ESP. How otherwise, for example, and to take a recently reported case, could a father be aware of his daughter being close to drowning when she is thousands of miles away?

Theories about ESP often evolve into theories about parapsychology's original concern, namely, whether there is any aspect of the human mind which survives death. In the final chapter I shall attempt to collate some of the modern experimental work on ASCs with some of the older psychic research on mediumship. Any resulting suggestions will of course be speculative, and although I have tried to include an optimum combination of speculation and hard core facts from research, the reader must remain free to form his own conclusions from the evidence.

2
Hypnosis and ESP

Hypnosis and extrasensory perception have traditionally been associated as important ingredients of occult phenomena. Trance states and psychic phenomena have always featured highly in the claims of the religious prophet, the shaman and the witchdoctor. But the parallels do not end with their occult ancestry, and attempts to study them scientifically show both to be elusive and difficult to predict or quantify. As with ESP, there is no generally accepted theory of hypnosis, neither is there a known way to measure it physiologically (Barber 1961), nor a definite relationship of hypnotic susceptibility to any personality dimension (Barber 1964). Moreover, in a similar manner to ESP research, hypnosis experiments often produce conflicting and contradictory findings, the important difference being that hypnotic phenomena are more easily accessible than paranormal events and therefore not so open to dispute. Nevertheless, it took over a hundred years for hypnosis to gain orthodox acceptance.

The history of mesmerism
Hypnosis first became recognised as a normal possibility, rather than 'possession by the devil' or an abnormal state, through the work of the Austrian physician Franz Anton Mesmer who lived in Paris during the late eighteenth and early nineteenth centuries. Mesmer put on public demonstrations of hypnosis in which much of his success could be attributed to his showmanship. Next to his patients he would place a large metallic bath filled with iron filings. They would be told that magnetic influences emanated from this and from the stars

and sun sewn on to his robes. Mesmer would then walk through the group of patients, touching them with metal rods, and this induced trances and hysteria.

Even as late as the mid-nineteenth century, magnetic and electrical influences were thought to be explanations for hypnosis. It was a case of understanding being retarded by the influence of the dominant sciences of the period.

In 1786 Luigi Galvani had shown that animal muscles could conduct and respond to electrical currents at the same time as Ampère, for example, was making important scientific discoveries in electricity and magnetism. A similar example of contemporary scientific bias may also be evident in the ill-fated attempts of our own day of trying to explain ESP in terms of wave theories. Even the later behavioural approach of attempting to relate ESP scores to precisely defined variables may be misguided, since new phenomena often require new approaches.

Another parallel between hypnosis and ESP lies in the hostile reaction of orthodox science to both. For a long time hypnosis was rejected as being nothing but fraud and imagination, until James Braid in 1841 produced an explanation that hypnosis was a form of 'nervous sleep'. Even then it did not gain much acceptance in medical circles. The medical journal *Lancet* once described hypnotic subjects as trained criminals who were paid for their acts, and it was only as recently as 1959 that the American Medical Association approved its use—and then only for medical practitioners.

At the time of Mesmer, psychic phenomena were allegedly a regular part of the somnambulist subject's repertoire. Mesmer wrote: 'Sometimes through his inner sensibilities the somnambulist can distinctly see the past and future,' and in illustration he demonstrated hypnosis from a distance to groups of observers. One of Mesmer's followers, the Marquis de Puységur, reported the use of hypnosis for medical diagnosis by clairvoyance. The British physicians Esdaile in India and Elliotson at London University also reported incidences of apparent hypnotic ESP. But even at that time, opinion was divided among hypnotists over the reality of the phenomena. Various committees in

France produced inconclusive or negative findings and the notable French hypnotist Bernheim wrote: 'I have in vain tried to induce a transmission of thoughts in hundreds of persons.' Yet despite initial failures, his colleague Liebault finally became convinced that clairvoyance was indeed a feature of hypnosis. Besides all this, it remains difficult to explain the differences between the present-day phenomena and those claimed by the mesmerists.

Nineteenth-century experiments in hypnosis and ESP

The experiments reported in the late nineteenth-century journals of the Society for Psychical Research (SPR) included three main types:

Hypnosis at a distance, being the apparent telepathic induction of hypnosis by the hypnotist.

Community of sensations, when the hypnotist experienced a certain taste or smell or was touched somewhere, and the subject reported the same experience.

Travelling clairvoyance, in which the subject was given suggestions to observe and report events occurring in some distant location.

The best-known examples of the apparent telepathic induction of hypnosis were the studies of the French psychiatrist Pierre Janet, carried out in 1885 and 1886 (Myers 1886, Gurney 1886). Observers included Charcot the neurologist and Frederick Myers of the SPR. Janet's subject Léonie waited in a house a quarter of a mile away where his housekeeper kept watch and recorded her waking and hypnotic states. In some cases an observer gave a signal for Janet to attempt to induce hypnosis at a distance and in others, random points of time on a clock were used. The results were very impressive, with fifteen successful attempts out of twenty-five on one occasion, and sixteen out of twenty on another.

Further work with Léonie was reported by the physiologist and Nobel prizewinner, Charles Richet. These were incidences of 'travelling clairvoyance'. Janet had instructed Léonie during hypnosis to observe Richet's Laboratory, and she correctly reported a fire before news could possibly have reached her by normal means. On another occasion, she was asked to describe what was happening to a colleague at a particular time, and again her report was said to be correct. She described him burning his hand with a brown liquid, which coincided with the time he had burnt his hand with bromine (Richet 1889).

A similar case was reported by the psychiatrist Alfred Backman of Kalmar in Sweden. This was the case of Alma Radberg to whom, without any preliminary arrangement (thereby removing expectancy as a possible explanation), it was suggested during 'travelling clairvoyance' that she appear to a 'target' person in Stockholm. She reported seeing a bunch of keys and Backman gave her instructions to draw the person's attention to it. It would seem that this was also successful, as he reported seeing an apparition of a woman drawing his attention to the keys on his desk (Backman 1891).

It is easy to dismiss the occasional case of this nature as due to deception, coincidence or inaccurate reporting, but the problem is that during that period there were many such instances. Other cases were reported by reputable investigators such as Eleanor Sidgwick (1891), Azam and Dufay (1889), and Augustus de Morgan, the logician. In addition to 'travelling clairvoyance', early SPR investigators found relatively easy success with 'community of sensations' experiments. When the hypnotist was touched, the subject responded as though he too had been touched (Podmore and Gurney 1884).

What can we make of these antiquated results? Eric Dingwall in an extensive coverage of earlier cases writes:

Experiments to them were not what we mean by the word. They were not systematic and we have no means of knowing whether detailed notes were made out at the time and how long after the observations the accounts were written. (Dingwall 1967.)

Certainly, by modern standards, insufficient details are given in the accounts to allow for critical examination or further investigation. Another difficulty is that nineteenth-century hypnotists used 'hysterics' as subjects, and by the mid-twentieth century hysteria had become rare as a diagnostic entity. Experimenters such as Rhine in the '30s used university subjects. Although there is little further work to confirm such findings, an exception can be found in the reports by John Björkhem, a Swedish psychiatrist, who also reported travelling clairvoyance during hypnosis. In one case the subject was told to visit her parent's house and was able to describe the scene in accurate detail including an item in the newspaper her father was reading. After the experiment her parents telephoned, full of anxiety because they were convinced they had seen her apparition (Björkhem 1942). Obviously interesting as such accounts are, they must remain anecdotal until more work is done. While it may be plausible to dismiss the whole thing as fraud or inaccurate reporting, one is left with a feeling that this cannot be the whole explanation. The answer could be that present-day researchers in hypnosis regard such phenomena with scepticism and little interest. Nineteenth-century superstition may have provided a cultural milieu within which such phenomena could occur, as there is much evidence that the form taken by hypnosis can be affected to a large degree by social, interpersonal and cultural factors. Consequently, the hypnosis of the nineteenth century may have differed crucially from the laboratory hypnosis of today, which raises the question of the fundamental nature of hypnosis.

Theories of hypnosis
Any theory of hypnosis has to explain a wide range of effects supposedly caused by it: catalepsy of limbs, hallucinations, regression of behaviour to earlier ages, apparently increased memory recall, analgesia, post-hypnotic effects and psychosomatic alterations. There are three main attempts at explanation of hypnosis; the psychoanalytic approach using Freudian concepts, an approach postulating hypnosis as an altered state of consciousness, and a behavioural approach rejecting concepts of hypnosis as a trance state, and formulating a description of the behaviour of the subject in terms of social variables.

The psychoanalytic orientation represented, for example, by Merton Gill and Margaret Brenman, sees hypnosis as explicable in terms of 'regression' and 'transference'. The subject's ego is regressed to an earlier stage of development in which his childhood needs and fantasies are 'transferred' onto the hypnotist, who becomes a father substitute. The problem with such theories is that, besides being difficult to test, they are often too general as explanations. Granted that we all have fantasies, needs and immature aspects, it is still difficult to understand why they are enhanced specifically in the hypnotic situation and how they can explain the whole range of effects.

The second main approach is to regard hypnosis as an altered state of consciousness, and importance here is attached to the subject's experience during hypnosis. Ernest Hilgard (1965), for example, in a description of the hypnotic state, lists subsidence of planning, redistribution of attention, fantasy production using past memories, tolerance for reality distortion, the playing of roles and, finally, amnesia for what transpired during hypnosis. Because there is no known correlate of hypnosis (or any other incontrovertible criterion), Tart and Hilgard have gone so far as to regard the subject's testimony of being hypnotised as being the criterion of hypnosis.

One may argue that the subject's report that he feels hypnotised to some degree is primary data about the presence or absence of hypnosis, if not a criterion of hypnosis. (Tart and Hilgard 1966.)

The behavioural approach to hypnosis is exemplified by Theodore Barber. His work is a critique of the whole methodology of research on hypnosis and the use of traditional concepts such as 'trance'. He argues that hypnosis is not a unitary phenomenon but is explicable in terms of five main variables relating to the demands of the situation upon the subject. Previous research on hypnosis had used the subjects as their own controls; that is, their performance in hypnosis had been compared with their performance in the normal waking state. Barber criticises this because subjects evidently have preconceptions about how they should perform when

39

hypnotised, and preconceptions become self-fulfilling. There-fore, Barber concludes, if one wants to demonstrate the effectiveness of a hypnotic state or 'trance', it is necessary to compare the performance of subjects in hypnosis with a separate group of waking subjects who are matched on all variables except the hypnotic trance-induction procedure. By applying this method, Barber has compared the performance of a task-motivated, waking group of subjects with a hypnotic induction group and found little or no difference. The method Barber and his co-workers use in 'task motivating' subjects is to give instructions stressing how easy it is to imagine and how the success of the experiment depends on their own willingness to succeed: 'Everyone passed these tests . . . if you try to the best of your ability to imagine, you can easily imagine and do the interesting things I tell you and you will be helping in this experiment and not wasting time.' (Barber and Calverley 1968.) Using this method, Barber and his co-workers have published about seventy reports during the last fifteen years in support of their belief that the same phenomena obtained through the use of hypnosis can be produced in a motivated waking state (Barber 1969). For example, in a recent investigation groups of subjects who had undergone a task-motivation and a hypnotic-induction procedure were compared on their ability to see an hallucinatory dog: 76 per cent of the task-motivated group and 68 per cent of the hypnotic group reported they had experienced a visual image of a dog. Moreover, the groups did not differ significantly in the location, vividness or stability of the image reported (Spanos, Ham, Barber 1973). Barber is also very critical of the use of the term hypnosis because he says it is circular to argue that subjects give high responses to suggestions because they are in a hypnotic state, and that we know they are in a hypnotic state because they give high responses to suggestions. Instead, Barber has produced experimental evidence that hypnosis can be conceptualised into 'antecedent' and 'consequent' variables. Although this division is somewhat suspiciously reminiscent of the stimulus-response analysis of 'rat psychology', his antecedent variables include factors of a subjective and interpersonal nature such as the attitudes and expectancies of the subject and experimenter, whether the situation is defined as hypnosis or not, and the subject's motivation for the task. The evidence produced by Barber and his co-workers suggested that these variables determine the subject's response to suggestions and his testimony of being hypnotised (Barber 1969).

Obviously, Barber's work is of enormous importance if he has succeeded in debunking beliefs of hypnosis as a trance or an altered state of consciousness, and in showing that it is explicable by social factors alone. His work, however, has not gone uncriticised.

Does a hypnotic trance exist? The Hilgard and Tart versus Barber and Calverley controversy

The controversy over whether hypnosis is an altered state of consciousness rests on two central issues. Is Barber correct in his methodology of using a separate control group of 'task-motivated subjects' with which to compare hypnotic subjects? Secondly, is Barber correct in assuming that a hypnotic trance (if it exists and has any effect on behaviour) can only be produced by a formal hypnotic induction procedure?

In 1966 at Stanford University, Hilgard and Tart reported two experimental studies in an attempt to show that Barber's approach was based on fallacious assumptions. They argued that using a separate control group was an insensitive design. Because there is a large amount of individual variation in hypnotic susceptibility, the few highly hypnotisable subjects in a group would have a marginal effect on the group's performance as a whole, and the group would therefore show little difference from a waking group. They attempted to demonstrate this by comparing two groups, a waking group which was told to imagine the suggestions and another which was given a formal hypnotic induction. The imagining group was also told to expect hypnosis:

Today you will be hypnotised and given a number of hypnotic tests. It has generally been found that exercising your imagination strongly in these experimental tasks produces a hypnotic state, even though we don't go through the formalities of hypnosis. The better you imagine, the more you'll respond. Try as hard as you can to concentrate and to imagine that the things I tell you are true. (Hilgard and Tart 1966.)

During the first session, the results of the tests of suggestibility showed no significant difference between the groups, but a second session was used where the imagining group received hypnosis as well. As expected, the results of the hypnotic group showed no significant change over their original performance, but the imagining group did show a significant difference from their previous waking performance. In opposition to Barber's view, Hilgard and Tart concluded from this that there was 'an effect to be attributed to hypnosis beyond the effect of motivating instructions'. Consistent and in support of the Hilgard and Tart view, there is in fact some evidence that only a few highly hypnotisable subjects produce a pronounced response to hypnosis. One very experienced hypnotist, Milton Erickson, worked exclusively with such subjects and found with hypnotically induced deafness that attempts to startle or even trick subjects into hearing failed. Dyne, another hypnotist, tried firing a gun unexpectedly, but even that produced no response. Erickson also found that subjects given negative hallucinations not to see certain objects would hurt themselves by walking into them (Erickson 1938). The point of these experiments, sadistic though they may sound, is to suggest that hypnosis can have an effect in a few sensitive subjects beyond what could reasonably be attributed to motivation.

The second point made by Tart and Hilgard in 1966 concerned whether Barber was correct or not in his initial assumption that a hypnotic state (if it exists) could only be produced by a formal induction procedure. In their first experiment Hilgard and Tart had used a 'state report' scale to assess the degree to which the subjects felt hypnotised. They found for *both* imagining and hypnotic groups that the scores on this scale correlated positively with the subject's performance on the suggestibility tests. (This did not appear to be due merely to the subject having given his estimate of hypnosis in accordance with knowledge of how well he had done on the tests, since state reports given *before* the tests also correlated with test scores.) (Hilgard and Tart 1966.) In a further investigation, Tart and Hilgard found that when they used a waking control group selected for their high suggestibility, but gave them instructions to stay awake, they became no longer highly suggestible. Their state reports indicated that in order to produce high scores on suggestibility tests they had to drift in hypnosis. This led Tart and Hilgard to conclude that subjects can enter hypnosis spontaneously whether or not they are given a formal hypnotic induction procedure (Tart and Hilgard 1966).

However, the controversy did not end there. In 1968 Barber and Calverley criticised Hilgard and Tart for using an imagining control group intead of comparing their hypnotic group with a waking group who were strongly motivated to succeed on the tests of hypnosis. But when Barber and Calverley repeated Hilgard and Tart's work, they actually obtained findings that seemed to confirm that hypnosis did have an effect beyond what could be obtained by the motivation to succeed alone. Rather than interpret this as being due to the presence of a hypnotic state, Barber and Calverley believe that it is due to the subjects' preconception of hypnosis as a situation in which they believe they can perform better. And yet it seems inconsistent that Hilgard and Tart's waking group, who believed they were being hypnotised, should score lower on tests than when they actually were hypnotised.

Finally, in 1969, Barber and Calverley reported another experiment. This time they asked subjects to close their eyes for five minutes and 'place themselves in hypnosis'. They then compared these subjects with those given a hypnotic induction on four dimensions of hypnotic behaviour: trance-like appearance, response to suggestion tests, reports of unusual experiences such as changes in body image, and the testimony of being hypnotised. There were no differences between the two groups over testimony of being hypnotised, nor over unusual experiences, but there was a small significant difference in trance-like appearance and test responses. They concluded: 'The statement "Place yourself in hypnosis" appears to be sufficient to produce most of the effects associated with formal hypnotic induction procedures.' Yet their results are reconcilable with Tart and Hilgard's. Barber and Calverley found for both groups that testimony of being hypnotised correlated strongly with, and produced the highest correlation with, the other dimensions of hypnosis. Furthermore, this intercorrelation accounted for 56 per cent of the variance in hypnotic behaviour. This suggests that a person's state of consciousness (that is, his testimony of being hypnotised or not) is probably the strongest determinant in hypnosis. Since this applies to 'waking' or 'imagining' groups, it may be that in a small percentage of the population a hypnotic state can occur spontaneously and is part of normal experience. Fortunately there is some more evidence which, while reconciling the major opponents in the controversy, also supports this view. This is the work of Martin Orne and Ronald Shor at Harvard University.

A three-dimensional theory

Ronald Shor has proposed a three-dimensional theory of hypnosis which corresponds to the aspects emphasised by the other main groups of exponents: Barber and Calverley, Hilgard and Tart, and Gill and Brenman. The three dimensions of hypnosis distinguished are hypnotic role-taking involvement, trance, and archaic involvement. Role-taking involvement includes aspects of hypnosis in line with Barber's variables— the subject's perception of the demands on him in the experimental situation, his motivation, etc. Trance is regarded as an altered state of consciousness 'in which the generalised reality-orientation has faded into relatively non-functional awareness'. The third concept, archaic involvement, is similar to the psychoanalytic notion of the 'transference' relationship with the hypnotist, but includes also the involvement of the total resources of the subject's personality. However, it is only in the deeper stages of hypnosis that there is any degree of trance and archaic involvement such that the hypnotist's suggestions become subjective reality. In agreement with Gill and Brenman, Shor believes that transference is particularly responsible for the classical phenomena of hypnosis such as age regression and repressed fantasies. It is plausible then that the experimental hypnosis of the laboratory is different from its clinical counterpart, since subjects there are more remote from the experimenter, compared with patients in a clinical setting. This could help to explain some of Barber's findings as well as the contrast between mesmerism and present-day hypnosis.

One of Shor's colleagues, Martin Orne, has studied the situational and trance aspects of hypnosis in more detail. He emphasises that subjects in psychology experiments (unlike physics, which is often the model for other scientific methods) actively respond to any implicit hints, the bias of the experimenter and the experimental situation in order to make the experiment a success. Orne calls this unwanted helpfulness a response to the 'demand characteristics' of the experiment. This is particularly important in hypnosis experiments where subjects will tend to take on the role of being hypnotised and behave as they believe they are expected to. An example of this is given by Orne when talking of the behaviour of subjects following a lecture-demonstration of hypnosis. Those who had seen a demonstration of spontaneous arm catalepsy as a (false) characteristic of hypnosis displayed it themselves when they became subjects, while those who had not seen the demonstration failed to display it. For this reason Orne advocates that experimenters should compare the effects of real hypnosis with those effects exhibited by subjects who are told to play at or simulate hypnosis. The experimenter is not told which are the hypnotic subjects and which the simulating ones, so that any differences are not due to his bias or 'demand characteristics'. Using this method, Orne found that only the hypnotic subjects displayed what he terms 'trance logic', the suspension of actual abilities and logical thought. Thus the hypnotised subject can tolerate inconsistencies such as being told to see an hallucinated image of a person and the real person together, while the simulating subject usually denies the existence of one of them in some way. Hypnotised subjects will also 'see' an hallucinated person through a chair and not be bothered by the incongruity (Orne 1959).

Shor and Orne consider that trance may be a constituent of other naturally occurring states rather than being confined to hypnosis, and they derived a scale, the 'Personal Experiences Questionnaire', to measure those hypnotic-like experiences. Questions concerned the frequency and intensity of dream, fantasy and mystical states. Examples from the Questionnaire are:

1   Have you ever had part of your body look strange and not like part of your body at all?
2   Have you ever found yourself staring at something and for the moment forgotten where you are?
3   Do you ever get seasick at ocean movies?
4   Have you ever had the experience of walking in your sleep?
5   Have you ever felt drunk while sober?
6   Have you ever become so absorbed when listening to music that you almost forgot where you are?
7   Have you ever felt a oneness with the universe, a melting into the universe or a sinking into eternity?
8   Have you ever been able to ignore pain?
9   Do you ever find yourself unwittingly adopting the mannerisms of other people?
10   Have you ever had the experience of seeming to watch yourself from a distance as if in a dream?

Shor, Orne and Connell (1962) found the intensity with which subjects reported these experiences correlated highly with hypnotic susceptibility measured by the Stanford Hypnotic Susceptibility Scale and it also gave a good prediction of the depth of hypnosis that subjects could reach. Prediction was actually best within the deeper stages of hypnosis and this led Shor, Orne and Connell to conclude that the trance component of hypnosis may only come into operation at this higher level while at lower levels the situational components (such as those stressed by Barber) are more effective.

Obviously these findings are crucial to a concept of hypnosis as an altered state of consciousness, and there is some confirmation by other experimenters. A questionnaire similar to Orne, Shor and Connell's was used by Ås (1962), and even Barber and Glass (1962) found that three items from their questionnaire correlated with suggestibility (although a later attempt by Barber and Calverley in 1965 failed to repeat this or those of Orne *et al.*). The three items were:

Do you like to read true stories about love and romance?
Do you find day dreaming very enjoyable?
When you were a child of about five or six did you have imaginary playmates who were rather vivid and almost real?

Sutcliffe, Perry and Sheeman (1970) reported by using a questionnaire that subjects who had more vivid imagery were more readily hypnotisable. They also found a measure of fantasy combined with vividness of imagery to give a good prediction of hypnotisability.

Hypnosis, then, seems to relate to personality in much the same way as ESP, and seems to be a function of the state of consciousness together with the interpersonal situation that is conducive to the phenomena. Consequently, the experimental finding that ESP occurs during hypnosis is one we would expect.

ESP during hypnosis

In trying to elucidate the relation of ESP to hypnosis, the problem of deciding how much is due to the subject's motivation and expectations during hypnosis also needs to be taken into account. This was evident from some of the earliest experimentation done in the late 1930s when J. B. Rhine dispensed with the use of hypnosis to induce ESP, preferring instead to work with a motivated waking state. Later he conceded: 'The general feeling we had at the Duke Laboratory was that we did not know what to tell the hypnotised subject to do to increase his powers' (Rhine 1952).

Charles Honorton and Stanley Krippner (1969) reviewed studies which compared ESP performance during hypnosis with the waking state. They found nine out of the twelve studies produced significant differences between the two states, but sometimes hypnosis would produce lower than chance and lower than the waking state. This may mean that hypnosis affects not the direction (psi hitting or missing) but the magnitude of the scores. Further, since four studies found significant differences without direct suggestions to score well, this implies that hypnosis has an effect beyond the explicit suggestion given. The question remains, however: Is the unknown factor the demand characteristics of the situation, the subject's expectation that hypnosis will enable him to score high, or some factor specific to the hypnotic *state*?

Honorton and Krippner favour the latter interpretation because, in his two studies, Honorton (1964, 1966) produced scores in hypnosis that were below chance and lower than the same subject's waking performance. This is contrary to subjects' prior expectations but in accord with the hypothesis that hypnosis affects the level of scoring but not whether it is significant above or below chance. However, in addition to this there is more direct evidence that ESP performance may be a function of a hypnotic state rather than suggestion, motivation or expectancy alone. These are studies which have used designs similar to those advised by Barber, and have compared the ESP scores of a hypnosis group with a group given an imagining task and/or motivating suggestions. All four studies (Casler 1962, Honorton 1969, Krippner 1968, Honorton 1972) produced evidence that the hypnosis performance was superior to that of groups given imagination-motivation instructions. However, in agreement with Barber, subjects who were motivated and told to imagine performed better than in their waking state (Honorton 1969). Considering the difficulty of repeating findings in parapsychology these findings show a remarkable degree of consistency. Honorton and Krippner conclude their survey by saying: 'It would appear that hypnosis provides one of the few presently available techniques for affecting the level of psi test performance.'

Why then is a hypnotic state apparently conducive to ESP?

Krippner reported that subjects given hypnosis produced their ESP scores in imagery after a rest period while the imagining group did not, instead incorporating their targets later into nocturnal imagery. He concluded that hypnosis may speed up the manifestation of the target into consciousness. Honorton, in an experiment on hypnotic dreams (1972) (to be described more fully in the next chapter), found that the highest ESP scores were produced by subjects who experienced the greatest *change* in their subjective state during hypnosis or the dream period. This finding is then in support of a shift in state hypothesis advanced in Chapter One.

A final consideration is that, accepting the existence of a trance state, it may be that the reduction of critical abilities during hypnosis makes us much more receptive to such apparently irrational phenomena as ESP. It may also explain the initial success of a method for developing psi ability proposed by the Czech parapsychologist Milan Ryzl.

The Ryzl technique
The basis of Ryzl's method involved three stages:

1 Intensive training, through hypnosis, in experiencing vivid, complex hallucinations.
2 Development of these hallucinations into vertical perceptions of targets for ESP. To do this subjects were encouraged to place themselves in a relaxed but concentrated state of mind.
3 The elimination of errors and then reduction of the dependence of the subject on hypnosis for success.

Using this method, Ryzl claimed he had success with about 10 per cent of his subjects but only one subject's performance was reported in detail. Some degree of credence can be given to his method, however, because this particular subject was Pavel Stepanek who, over the last ten years, has given a stable and steady performance with several investigators (Pratt 1973). Stepanek is also important because it was through this work that a new aspect of ESP was revealed; its associative links with objects. Stepanek had begun by identifying the colours of randomly selected cards sealed in envelopes, but soon after this his responses began to be focused onto the envelopes themselves; he would consistently give a specific response to a specific envelope. This looked at first to be just normal sensory learning, but Stepanek did not see the cards which he associated with the envelopes and furthermore he continued to produce this 'focusing effect' when the envelopes were themselves covered by jackets (Ryzl and Pratt 1963) (Pratt and Ransom 1972). The focusing effect suggests that ESP can work like memory in forming associations, and is an experimental analogue of what mediums claimed to do in giving 'clairvoyant readings' from personal objects.

Since Ryzl's publications it has always been a controversial matter whether or not his success was incidental to his hypnotic technique and due only to his 'luck' in discovering a few high-scoring subjects. The three or four attempted duplications of Ryzl's technique all failed to yield anything conclusive (Stephenson 1965, Edmunds and Jolliffe 1965, Beloff and Mandelberg 1966), although all attempts to replicate it have failed to include some major aspect such as the high degree of hallucinatory experience, and all have used too small a sample of subjects. More serious than any of this is Ryzl's own failure to consolidate his earlier claims since he went to work in the United States.

Whether or not this is the repeatable technique for ESP induction that parapsychologists have been looking for, what the Ryzl technique does seem to illuminate is the importance of the two sets of factors discussed previously, interpersonal factors such as the subject's motivation, his relationship with the experimenter and his expectancies, and the subject's state of consciousness. Both sets of factors may apply to ESP as well as to hypnosis, and variations in their presence may be an explanation for some of the contradictions in research and failure of replications. Ryzl worked with a few of his subjects over a long period of time, building up a high degree of expectancy and confidence in success as well as suggesting to them that they should experience a relaxed, receptive state of consciousness.

The manifestation of the more 'unusual' phenomena of hypnosis may depend crucially on the interaction of these factors. These unusual phenomena include secondary personalities, out-of-the-body experiences, psychedelic effects and hypnotic dreams. They suggest that hypnosis may merge into other states of consciousness, and that distinctions between ASCs are somewhat arbitrary.

Hypnosis and other ASCs

A feature of many ASCs is the appearance of secondary personalities masquerading as reincarnation. Many such cases appear to reveal a higher degree of knowledge than the waking personality was capable of, as well as being in dramatic contrast. Because of this, cases like those of Bridey Murphy, Patience Worth and the Three Faces of Eve have gained publicity. This is also a feature of hypnosis, that after suggestions to the subject to revert to a time before birth, another personality may emerge. Often an explanation can be offered in terms of repressed or undeveloped parts of the self. Edwin Zolek (1962) gives such a case for which a psychoanalytic explanation seemed appropriate.

The subject had produced a reincarnation fantasy of being Brian O'Malley, a British officer killed by a horsefall. Further analysis suggested that the fantasy represented in a symbolic way the subject's unresolved conflict with his grandfather. When he was young, his grandfather had regaled him with stories of his army days, including tales of a hated officer called O'Malley who had in fact been killed by falling from a horse. The subject had later lost his grandfather's affection and had been punished by him for using a horse. Thus the O'Malley fantasy became a way of symbolising the subject's hostility towards his grandfather, but it remains to explain why there is a need to invent secondary personalities, even if one can explain their form. C. T. K. Chari (1958) has suggested there may be a childhood fantasy of a magical death-life cycle which is rejuvenated by hypnosis. When asked what happens to dead people, children will often give evidence of this by saying, for example, 'they go back into their Mummy's tummy and become a baby again'. The problem is that in the more highly developed cases the degree of creativity that can be reached often seems to transcend the knowledge of the person involved. John Björkhem (1942) reported being able to induce many such instances in his subjects through hypnosis. Many cases contrasted convincingly with the waking personality and acted out dramas and scenes relating to their alleged life times. Particularly impressive are alleged linguistic abilities that the new personality seems to possess, which are not part of the person's conscious learning. Björkhem concluded that explanations were premature and that 'the phenomena everywhere move in the outskirts of what the human psyche is credited with'. Whatever the explanation, such cases are important because they indicate that the organism has a much greater range of resources than is usually thought. An explanation will probably help to elucidate another class of phenomena with which there is an obvious overlap, that of the trance personalities of mediumship.

As well as mediumistic trance, hypnosis has a transition with other ASCs illustrated by cases of psychedelic-like experiences and out-of-the-body experiences reported during hypnosis.

Bernard Aaronson (1965) has described how, by altering the subject's perception of depth, space and time through hypnotic suggestion, he was able to induce quite dramatic changes in personality varying from schizophrenic-like experiences—when suggestions were given for these dimensions to be contracted—to psychedelic-like experiences—when suggestions of expansion were given. Aaronson concluded that personality is not constant except under limited perceptual conditions.

Tart (1968) reported that by using a technique of mutual hypnosis psychedelic-like effects can be produced. Here the two subjects were also hypnotists and induced hypnosis in each other under the direction of Tart. The effects were dramatic and included changes in body image, self perception and even a merging of their respective identities. Shared fantasies and apparent telepathic communication of these were also experienced. In fact, when hypnosis was successfully used with LSD to guide and control the experience along therapeutic lines the results have been effective (Levine and Ludwig 1966). Findings such as these seem to suggest that a much higher degree of self exploration can be reached when consciousness is altered than in waking consciousness, and the paranormal aspect to such experiences adds credence to the validity of subjective experiences.

There are three major points that seem to emerge from all this work. First, hypnosis seems to be an altered state of consciousness in which 'inner reality' predominates. The findings of Martin Orne and Ronald Shor indicate that such states may occur naturally and in agreement with the findings of Tart and Aaronson that hypnosis may afford a transition to other ASCS. Secondly, the extensive experimentation by Theodore Barber emphasises how important motivational, expectancy and inter-personal factors are in the occurrence of hypnotic phenomena. This is, of course, consistent with what has been said earlier about demand characteristics and experimenter effects. Finally, the hypothesis of a relation between ASCS and ESP finds further backing from hypnosis research. A moderate degree of repeatability has been reached in using hypnosis to induce ESP effects. As to the nature of this relationship, Ryzl's description of the psi-conducive state is in agreement with the description given by high-scoring ESP subjects (White 1964)—that of relaxed concentration. Completing the picture is the fact that Rhine noticed that many of his high-scoring subjects appeared to be in a trance-like state. This is particularly consistent with Tart and Hilgard's findings that a small number of subjects could spontaneously enter trances during experimentation, and it may be from this group that many successful ESP subjects are drawn.

Thus, hypnosis seems to illustrate the potent effect of the two main factors that we hypothesised in the previous chapter. Probably its success in producing a wide range of experiences is that it can maximise both these interpersonal and subjective state factors.

3
Trance Mediumship

One of the most fascinating but equally enigmatic states of consciousness is the trance of mediumship. An obvious source of evidence in support of a link between ESP and altered states of consciousness, it offers at the same time a wealth of other claims which, while they cannot be verified, cannot be easily dismissed. Certainly the first impression may be to reject a great part of the phenomenon as fraud, superstition or deception, although there does seem to be a basis in veridical phenomena beyond this.

The public image of the séance room largely derives from that of physical mediumship. The rising table, the issuing forth of sheets of drapery as spirit ectoplasm, and voices of the dead bellowing forth from trumpets, all these belong to physical mediumship. In the present chapter I am giving myself the relatively easy task of concentrating on mental mediumship rather than its more dubious physical counterpart. It is in mental mediumship that the medium enters a trance and claims to become possessed by a 'spirit' relaying messages from the dead.

In common with other states of consciousness like hypnosis, mediumship has occult origins. Frank Podmore in his book *Modern Spiritualism* (1902) attributes the rise of mediumship in the nineteenth century to the popularity of mesmerism, phrenology and other pseudo sciences, coupled with the religious fervour of that time. Indeed, the form and content of ASCs seem to be dictated by cultural influences; so much so that by the 1970s mediumship is almost dying out.

Fortunately, two gifted mediums, Mrs Piper and Mrs

Leonard, have been the subject of extensive study over a period of years by the Society for Psychical Research (SPR) and a third, Mrs Eileen Garrett, has received more recent investigation, albeit less extensive.

In accounting for the material produced by mediums, four explanations are usually considered, the most obvious being deception. Another explanation in terms of normal processes is whether the medium's conscious or unconscious use of non-verbal hints or subliminal cues could give rise to apparent veridical messages. Thirdly, if we grant the existence of ESP, it may be that the medium in her trance plays the role of the deceased personality and uses ESP from the living to perfect the impression. Finally, there is the view that the messages are what they claim to be, spirit communication.

Investigations of mediums by the Society for Psychical Research

Certainly the hypothesis of fraud or deception seems inapplicable to either Mrs Piper or Mrs Leonard. Mrs Piper was studied constantly by the Society for Psychical Research during the period 1886 to 1911—Richard Hodgson being sent out to Boston for this purpose—and nothing suspicious ever arose. Having first impressed the eminent American psychologist, William James, she continued to produce veridical communications, even when Sir Oliver Lodge invited her to England to be investigated by detectives.

Use of subliminal and non-verbal cues did not seem a viable explanation either, since she would often show knowledge of events about which no one present knew anything, as was the case with the Uncle Jerry incident. Lodge gave Mrs Piper a watch belonging to a deceased uncle which she correctly identified as belonging to Uncle Jerry. She then went on to recall an odd collection of his boyhood events, including the killing of a cat in Smith's Field, owning a snake skin and being nearly drowned in a creek, all of which seemed correct. The twin brother of the deceased uncle verified the snake skin statement and another uncle recollected both the killing of the cat and the creek incident. The uncles, of course, may have had memories which conveniently complied with Lodge's wishes, but besides Lodge, Mrs Piper satisfied other investigators of first-class ability.

The initial investigation was conducted by Frederick Myers, Walter Leaf and Richard Hodgson and William James as well as Lodge. James, Hodgson and Leaf were all highly sceptical initially, but came to the opinion that she produced material quite beyond what she could have acquired through normal channels. Hodgson was particularly impressed by one of Mrs Piper's controls, George Pelham, who claimed to be a deceased friend of his. Sitters attended anonymously and yet the Pelham control responded with the appropriate memories and gestures, and picked thirty of his friends from the 150 strangers without mistake. Events then took an unexpected twist. Hodgson himself died suddenly and shortly afterwards he, or his impersonation, began communicating through Mrs Piper. William James, who had been a close friend of Hodgson's, was given the task of assessing the credentials of this 'spirit' Hodgson. The difficulty was that Mrs Piper had also known Hodgson over a period of years, and it was therefore possible that she could easily effect an impersonation of him, albeit unconsciously, during the trance. James, after an intensive study of this 'Hodgson', concluded: 'I myself feel as if an external will to communicate were probably there; that is, I find myself doubting, in consequence of my whole acquaintance with that sphere of phenomena, that Mrs Piper's dream life, even equipped with "telepathic" powers, accounts for all the results found. But if asked whether the will to communicate be Hodgson's, or some mere spirit counterfeit of Hodgson, I remain uncertain and await more facts, facts which may not point clearly to a conclusion for fifty or a hundred years.'

That was written by America's foremost psychologist at the time, and almost seventy years later it is still uncertain where such evidence points. In the end it has become a choice between an explanation involving unconscious dramatisation supplemented by extrasensory perception, and a hypothesis involving survival of some form. Eleanor Sidgwick, writing a paper in 1915 on the psychology of Mrs Piper's trance, concluded in favour of the former hypothesis: 'I think it is probably a state of self-induced hypnosis in which her hypnotic self personates different characters, either consciously and deliberately, or unconsciously, believing herself to be the person she represents and also using fragmentarily telepathic impressions.' Further support for this viewpoint is a test case by the psychologist Stanley Hall who asked to be put into contact with an imaginary niece, 'Bessie Beals', and obligingly the 'Hodgson' control introduced a 'Bessie Beals'.[1] Some of Mrs Piper's controls were evidently fictitious dramatisations—her main control was named Phinuit, a French doctor who knew very little medicine and even less French, and other characters included a Julius Caesar, a Walter Scott and a George Eliot, all of whom talked nonsense most of the time. William James in a less charitable frame of mind wrote: 'If the great minds of this world degenerate so much on death, the outlook for lesser fry is bleak.'

So far then, mediumship as revealed by the Piper material seems explicable in terms of impersonation during the trance state with access to the necessary information being gained through ESP. This receives support from the evidence (reviewed in Chapter Two) which suggests that hypnotic states are receptive to ESP, but some reservation must be made since there is little data on which to assume a similarity or identity of the hypnotic and mediumistic trances. Mediumship appears to have much in common wth secondary personality, but this will be discussed in more detail when we have seen how the impersonation-ESP hypothesis has to be modified to encompass the material produced by the other great medium, Mrs Osborne Leonard.

[1] However, Fraser Nicol has recently pointed out that Stanley Hall was less than frank about this incident and 'there was indeed a person, Bessie Beals, who was not without significance in this matter'. See F. Nicol, 'The Usefulness of History', *Research in Parapsychology 1972*, edited by W. G. Roll (Scarecrow Press, Metuchen N.J. 1973). I am indebted to Professor J. Beloff for this information.

Mrs Leonard was studied by the SPR for forty years, and fraud or deception seem inapplicable. Besides incidents of apparent ESP from those present at a sitting, Mrs Leonard could often produce material which appeared to be outside the knowledge of those present, suggesting a much wider form of ESP. One of the well-known examples of this concerned the death of Sir Oliver Lodge's son, Raymond, during the First World War. Mrs Leonard's control personality, Feda, described a group photograph giving details of numbers and Raymond's position in relation to the man behind him. In fact, such a photograph arrived some weeks after his death, sent by the mother of a brother officer.

Other instances suggestive of ESP are the 'book tests'. Here the control personality would attempt to identify what was written in a particular book from a bookshelf she was unacquainted with, specifying the page and line number. The results analysed by Mrs Eleanor Sidgwick gave 17 per cent correct, and 17 per cent approximately correct, while a control series of random matchings gave only 2 per cent correct and 3 per cent approximately so. However, these were subjective estimates and therefore open to bias. The most impressive examples of ESP which ruled out the use of non-verbal and subliminal cues, or even ESP, from those immediately present, were obtained by the use of 'proxy sittings'. The early investigators into survival after death used to argue the pros and cons of the rival theories—ESP from those present versus genuine 'spirit' communication. To reduce the possibility that the medium was tapping the minds of the sitters, it would be arranged for someone to attend on his behalf. A good example of such a proxy sitting was that arranged by Professor E. R. Dodds (Thomas 1939) for a Mrs Lewis who wished to communicate with her father, a Mr Macauley. The sitting was held by the Reverend Drayton Thomas who did not know Mrs Lewis personally. As evidence of identity, the trance Macauley described his working instruments, tool chest, mathematical formulae, drawing office and his pet name for his daughter, Puggy. He also said he had a damaged hand and named some friends of his, one of whom was named as Reece but 'sounds like Riss'. Baths were also said to be important. All this proved correct, including his daughter's name. Macauley had been a water engineer and his anxiety about not wasting water had been a family joke. Furthermore, her father had hero-worshipped an older boy called Rees who had made a point of his name being pronounced 'Reece not Riss' to the extent that his sisters used to tease him. In all, Drayton Thomas estimated that out of the 124 statements made, fifty-one were 'correct', twelve were 'good', thirty-two 'fair' and twenty-nine 'failures'. Therefore, to explain this kind of success we have to at least evoke a 'super ESP hypothesis' that the process can operate over long distances and acquire selective information from specific persons. This appeared more incredible thirty or forty years ago than it does now. Recently we have had experiments involving ordinary subjects showing that this kind of selective access is possible (Osis and Carlson 1972, Krippner, Honorton, Ullman 1972). If we think of mind and ESP in terms of physical energy concepts, there undoubtedly are problems; memories are not arranged in a neat filing system for systematic telepathic selection. Instead, it seems more useful to assume that consciousness has its own laws such as those of associational and emotional linkage by which ESP may operate (Stanford 1973). An example of this seemed to occur with one of Mrs Piper's controls, Sir Walter Scott, who made his debut the day after Hodgson had been reading a book by him.

If we must assume these propositions, then the 'super ESP hypothesis' seems to explain most of the phenomena without recourse to disembodied spirits. This leaves the 'impersonation' aspect of mediumship to be accounted for, and for this, clinical cases of secondary personality are particularly illuminating.

Secondary personality

In these cases consciousness is dissociated into two or more autonomous selves, often representing repressed or opposite aspects of personality. Mediumship may reflect the same principle, with trance personality being a split-off ancillary

59

self which assumes the role of a deceased personality. However, it must be stressed that cases of secondary personality are pathological while there is no suggestion of this in mediumship.

Secondary personality seems, like mediumship, to be much rarer today. W. S. Taylor and M. F. Martin in 1944 listed seventy-six such cases, but even then most cases were old and today secondary personality is almost extinct from the psychiatric literature. As with hypnosis and hysteria it may be that culture has a determining effect on the form of psychological phenomena. Today's society is probably much less overtly repressive and therefore cases of split-off personality are rarer. The most publicised recent case is, of course, 'The Three Faces of Eve' reported by Corbett Thigpen and Hervey Cleckley (1957). 'Eve White' had come to them complaining of headaches which seemed to be a psychosomatic expression of her conflicts with her husband over sex and religion. Her psychiatrists found her to be a dull, staid, moral woman and when a second personality suddenly emerged it seemed to be a manifestation of her repressed half; this 'Eve Black' was seductive, outrageous and domineering. Whereas 'Eve White' was completely oblivious of the other, 'Eve Black' claimed to know all 'White's' thoughts and was outrightly contemptuous of them, so much so that, when it was time for the two personalities to alternate, Eve Black would for example get drunk and leave White with the hangover! Eventually a third personality emerged, Jane, who seemed to be an integration of the other two. This was also an informative case because studies were made of the personalities using an EEG and psychological tests. Eve Black could be distinguished from White from the EEG records, and from her responses on the semantic differential (a test of the relation between concepts a person has of himself and others), which showed all three personalities to have completely separate structures. Some insight into the possible dynamics of the case was given when the fourth and final personality emerged as the re-integration of the other three. She related a childhood trauma of being forced to touch her dead grandmother's face at the funeral. As a tentative explanation, Thigpen and Cleckley suggested that this experience may have given her a fear of death and a wish to avoid it by creating the good virtuous self of 'Eve White', while at the same time compensating for her helplessness by forming the more domineering self of 'Eve Black'.

Whatever the explanation, it is a common feature in such cases for there to be a direct contrast between the personalities, to the extent that they are opposed to each other.

An example which seems very similar to the Eve case is that of Sally Beauchamp, 'Sally' being frivolous and irresponsible and playing tricks on the other personality, staid and conventional 'Christine Beauchamp' (M. Prince 1905). Cases like these seem most easily understood in terms of Jungian psychology. Carl Jung proposed that the unconscious was composed of both personal and collective layers. The latter becomes expressed in 'archetypical forms', many of which symbolise opposite or complementary parts of the self, and if one pole is developed at the expense of the other then conflict and autonomous expression of it result. The pious saint who has dreams of rape, seduction and violence would be a good example of this. It was Jung who coined the terms introversion and extraversion for describing those who have a preoccupation with inner world and outer world respectively. Important archetypes include the 'persona' or social self we display to the world, and the 'shadow' which is more primitive and repressed, the darker side of man. The main difficulty involved in this formulation (besides its lack of empiricism) is the tendency to indulge in talk of entities, structures and repressed parts, rather than viewing them as potential forms of experience. Consciousness is a process, contrary to the famous analogy of consciousness and the unconscious as an iceberg part surfaced and part submerged.

How much resemblance do the trance personalities of mediumship have with multiple personality? Unfortunately there has been little work done to answer this, although a study by Whateley Carington (1939) seems to suggest that there was some resemblance. The Word Association Test devised by

61

Jung was administered to the mediums Mrs Osborne Leonard, Rudi Schneider and Eileen Garrett. The method compared the dominant 'control' personality and the waking personality on their reaction times to the words. Results indicated a small negative correlation between the two personalities, not something one would expect from testing two different people or the same person twice, but more in accord with opposite, complementary personalities. Carington's work suffered from some statistical flaws and it is unfortunate that no mediums of comparable calibre are available today to permit a repetition of his work and the application of other psychological tests.

Another feature which lends support to the idea of a similarity between trance mediumship and secondary personality is a corresponding occurrence of emotional trauma during childhood. Alain Assailly (1963) in a case study of ten mediums reported that four had had violent fathers, and many had had emotional problems with their parents, difficult adolescent periods and unhappy marriages. While this may of course apply equally well to a large section of society, it is interesting to notice that Mrs Leonard traced the origin of her mediumship to the shock of discovering death as a child when she saw a funeral and asked about it. Mrs Piper's interest in mediumship also resulted after she had gone to a faith healer, following a 'personal accident'.

While both mediumship and secondary personality may involve some kind of emotional disturbance, the essential difference seems to be that whereas secondary personality involves a pathological splitting of the unaccepted parts of personality, the splitting in mediumship is aimed at performing a benevolent function—taking the role of the deceased person in order to console the bereaved. This allows the medium's waking personality to retain its integrity and to disown responsibility for failures of the 'spirit control'. The split is often so extreme that it is common for the waking personality, in cases of secondary personality and trance mediumship, to be unaware of the thoughts and actions of the ancillary one and (although reports are not explicit on this) to have amnesia for that period. This seemed to be true of Mrs Leonard and Mrs Piper, while Mrs Garrett sometimes reported mystical experiences during that period. Obviously it is crucial to any view which quotes mediumship as evidence for survival of personality to know whether there is 'co-consciousness' of the medium's personality with the trance personality, or whether it undergoes a change rather similar to playing the role of another person.

Just how trance consciousness can produce an impersonation of a deceased person is illustrated by the Gordon Davis case. In 1922 the British parapsychologist S. G. Soal was having sittings with the medium Blanche Cooper when a voice claimed to be 'Gordon Davis from R-R-Roch'. Soal recognised this as an old school friend from his school, Rochford, whom he believed had been killed during the First World War. Gordon Davis went on to try and prove his identity by referring to mutual experiences like his habit of arguing with his Geography teacher and their last conversation about guard duties. Although this impressed Soal there was some possibility the medium had picked up sub-vocal cues provided by him, although what followed could not be explained in this way.

Five days later 'Gordon Davis' described his house: 'Something about a funny dark tunnel—to do with his house—there are five or six steps and a half?' The house was 'joined up to others—don't think it's a proper street—like half a street— get the letter "E". There's something right in front of his house—not a veranda—something that's not in front of other houses'. Inside the house were 'a very large mirror and lots of pictures—all scenes—glorious mountains and the sea—some vases—very big ones with funny saucers—downstairs there are two funny brass candlesticks—on a shelf—black dickie bird— on the piano. There's a woman—and little boy—fond of the country—think it's his wife' (quoted in West 1962). Although Soal had thought Gordon Davis long dead, he was in fact alive and well and living in Southend. Three years after the sittings when Soal went to visit him, he found he was living at 54 Eastern Esplanade (hence the 'E's). There were six steps up to the door but one was a thin slab; it was a terraced house facing the sea with no houses on that side ('like half a street'). Furthermore, a tunnel passed from the front street to the back garden, and on the other side of the street in front of the house was a sea shelter. The contents of the house also tallied. There was a very large mirror and seven pictures, every one of scenery with mountains or sea in six of them. There were five large vases, two saucer-shaped china plaques, a small ornament of a kingfisher on the piano, and downstairs on a mantelshelf were two brass candlesticks. Gordon Davis had a wife and a boy aged five. Evidently, this was more than chance co-incidence, and to explain it we must suppose that the medium had used precognitive (prophetic) abilities because the real Gordon Davis did not move into the house until a year after the fake Davis described it and much of the ornamentation arose fortuitously.

A case such as this gives plausibility to the 'impersonation-ESP theory'. Indeed, and but for one class of phenomena, there would be little need to give any credence at all to the claims of mediumship in demonstrating survival after death. This class of phenomena is known as the 'cross correspondences'.

The cross correspondences

If there is anything to the claims of mediumship, one could ask: 'What happens when the researchers themselves die? Do they personally give any better evidence of survival or attempt to resolve any of the contradictions involved in such beliefs?'

Several of the leading SPR scholars died at the turn of the century, Edmund Gurney in 1888, Henry Sidgwick in 1900 and Frederick Myers in 1901. A few weeks after Myers's death, Mrs Verrall, lecturer in classics at Newnham College, Cambridge, and a friend of Myers, began producing automatic writing. This is a technique where the person writes without thinking of or looking at the words and thus is unaware of what has been written until it is read. This usually produces, if anything, an incoherent mixture of fantasies, which seemed to be so with Mrs Verrall's scripts, except that they were signed by

'Myers'. The interesting thing was that at this time Mrs Piper in America began making allusions in her trance to some of the material in the Verrall scripts. The reverse also happened. On 28th January 1902, for example, Richard Hodgson suggested to Mrs Piper's control that he should try to appear to Mrs Verrall's daughter (who had also begun writing) holding, of all things, a spear in his hand. The control misheard this as 'sphere' and was corrected, but the error persisted, for on 4th February, while claiming to be successful, he spelled the word 'sphear'. As it happened the message seemed to reach Mrs Verrall and not her daughter, for on 31st January Mrs Verrall, although receiving no visual impression, wrote a script containing the Greek for sphere and Latin for spear. It seemed unlikely that such a correspondence could have arisen by chance and, even if we allow for ESP, we are still left with the question of who effected the translation, since Mrs Piper knew no Greek or Latin.

Soon other automatists were involved. In India, Mrs Alice Fleming, the sister of Rudyard Kipling, began trying automatic writing and obtained scripts also signed 'Myers' but telling her to send them to Mrs Verrall's address. The correct address was given and apparently Mrs Fleming (known to the literature as 'Mrs Holland') could not have known this by normal means. In the end six or seven persons were involved, all producing a series of literary quotations, allusions, references to Greek mythology and anagrams which seemed to refer to each other's scripts. Often the messages made no sense taken separately, but together they appeared to form a jigsaw puzzle of associations, and the scripts themselves implied that this was the intention. Mrs Verrall's 'Myers' wrote: 'Record the bits and when fitted they will make the whole.' 'I will give the words between you; neither alone can read but together they will give the clue he wants' (Saltmarsh 1938). Moreover, instructions were often given to send the script to the automatist or investigator to whose script it alluded. As Rosalind Heywood (1966) notes, the material was experimenting on itself, but the question remains as to who thought out the jigsaw.

Unfortunately, many of the scripts require specialised classical knowledge but the 'Thanatos Case' is a simpler example. On 17th April 1907 Mrs Piper said what sounded like Sanatos, repeated as Tanatos. On 23rd April it was correctly pronounced 'Thanatos', the Greek for death. This was repeated three times on 30th April and on 7th May 'I want to say Thanatos' appeared. Meanwhile, on April 16th in India Mrs Fleming had written: 'Maurice Morris Mors—And with that the shadow of death fell upon his limbs'. Possibly Maurice and Morris were first attempts at Mors, but whatever the case, Mors is the Latin for death. Next, Mrs Verrall's script of 29th April said: 'Warmed both hands before the fire of life. It fades and I am ready to depart,' which was followed by a drawing of a triangle, or the Greek letter delta, a sign for death. Then the words 'Manibus date lilia plenis' (Latin for 'Give lilies with full hands') were written together with 'Come away, come away, Pallida mors' (Latin for pale death). Finally, it was stated explicitly: 'You have got the word plainly written all along in your own writing. Look back.' 'Manibus date lilia plenis' is from the *Aeneid* where Andrises foretells the death of Marcellus, and 'Come away, come away' is from Shakespeare, the next word being 'death' (Saltmarsh 1938). Again, chance seems an unlikely explanation and fraud or deception even less likely, considering the reputations and numbers of people involved. Even ESP seems too simple an explanation because many of the cases are much more complex and appear to follow a plan; some even seem intentionally designed as difficult puzzles. It was claimed that the communicators thought out this scheme in order to circumvent any such explanation in terms of ESP from the living. Certainly the idea was a persistent one for the cross correspondences. It went on for thirty years and occupied many thousands of pages in the *Journal* and *Proceedings* of the SPR.

What explanation is there for the cross correspondences? How can we reconcile the evidence of identity revealed in them with the hard facts of neurophysiology which tell us the mind is merely a function of the brain? Alter the brain by drugs or injury and personality vanishes or changes out of recognition. Many solutions have been attempted by experts (Broad 1962, Price 1953, Murphy 1952), but most of them have proved untestable. We need to know much more about the process of extrasensory, acquired knowledge and how it relates to consciousness. Some recent experiments by Rex Stanford of the University of Virginia have suggested that ESP may have an influence on our associations and that this can occur quite unconsciously. Stanford asked students to listen to a simulated dream report and then asked questions about it. In fact, the 'correct' answers were not specified in the text but chosen from several alternatives by a random means. Subjects chose their answers from these alternatives and an analysis of their scores in relation to their response biases indicated that some subjects had gained extrasensory knowledge of the 'correct' answers (Stanford 1970). A similar effect was also shown to operate in word association (Stanford 1973). From such experiments then, we might expect ESP to occur during free association such as the automatic writing of the cross correspondences.

Another approach to the problem of trance communications is that used by the Cambridge philosopher, the late C. D. Broad. Broad produced a masterly review of the mediumship of Mrs Leonard and Mrs Willett[1] in 1962 which is in accord with methods recommended by Tart in studying ASCs. This is to try to understand the experimental world of the trance communicators and evaluate it relative to that state of consciousness. It is Broad's article I refer to next.

The psychology and phenomenology of mediumship
If we accept for heuristic purposes that the experiences described by the communicators are subjectively valid, what do they tell us about survival after death and the process of communication? As Broad remarks, if they are who they claim to be we could not have better experts.

However, something needs to be said first about the states of

[1] This was her pseudonym; she was really Mrs Coombe-Tennant.

consciousness involved in mediumship and what the mediums themselves experienced. Professional mediums such as Mrs Leonard and Mrs Piper enter trance by progressive relaxation and then personal controls. In these cases 'Feda' and 'Phinuit' are alleged to take possession of the medium's brain and act as a liaison for contact with other 'spirits'. Sometimes these 'spirits' claim to take direct control of the medium. With the exception of Mrs Piper, the others involved in the cross correspondences used automatic writing. Unfortunately, psychologists have almost totally ignored the study of automatic writing despite its implications for both normal and abnormal psychology. In principle it appears to resemble the well-known automatism in which hands are placed on a glass around which are arranged the letters of the alphabet. The movements of the glass then spell out messages. This often merely reflects unconscious muscular movements in the hands in response to the questions, but in the automatic writing of the cross correspondences, most of the participants seemed to be in an ASC. For example, Mrs Verrall writes: 'I am sometimes exceedingly sleepy during the production of the writing and more than once I have momentarily lost consciousness of my surroundings.' Mrs Fleming also had difficulty in retaining awareness of her surroundings and avoiding a deep trance (Saltmarsh 1938).

Another automatist involved in the cross correspondences was Mrs Willett, and it is from Mrs Willett and Mrs Leonard that we got most of the descriptions of the discarnate state. Mrs Willett was the antithesis of the image of mediums as hysterics or demented old ladies, as she belonged to Victorian high society. She experienced several states of consciousness in producing her material, a waking state in which automatic writing was produced, a 'daylight state' in which she was awake and felt to be in verbal contact with the communicators, a dream state and a trance state. But Mrs Willett never experienced a 'possession' state like that of Mrs Piper and Mrs Leonard, in which her personality was displaced. In the trance state, hallucinations of the communicators occurred, while in the lighter stages it was more a feeling of presence. The main communicators were again the SPR researchers Gurney, Myers and Sidgwick. Often Mrs Willett produced excursions into Greek and philosophical writings which seemed quite beyond her normal knowledge. As C. D. Broad notes, 'Surely it *is* very surprising indeed that anything of this kind should come from a lady so completely uninterested and ignorant of philosophy as Mrs Willett, and that it should be couched in language and dramatic form so characteristic of the persons ostensibly communicating'[1] (Broad 1962).

What then did these ostensible communicators 'Gurney', 'Myers' and 'Sidgwick' say about the process they used? They claimed to use the subliminal (subconscious) mind of Mrs Willett, allowing ideas to 'incubate' or 'crystallise' by 'weaving' through her unconscious. It is interesting with respect to this that although information is occasionally produced which is outside the normal knowledge of the person, this is more rare. Thus Greek and Latin are more often used when the automatist is familiar with the language. When they do appear with mediums such as Mrs Leonard or Mrs Piper who knew no Greek or Latin, they are often accompanied by errors or alliterations. The previous example of Mrs Piper apparently mistaking Sanatos for Thanatos illustrates this. This might suggest that communication was somewhat limited by the verbal knowledge and associations of the medium, which is in further agreement with indications from experimental studies that ESP works by use of associations of ideas.

We now turn to the second question of what the communicators say about their own conscious state, be it discarnate and post-mortem or not. They conceive of the mind as a three-part structure composed of a 'supraliminal self', a 'subliminal self' and a 'transcendental self'. The supraliminal self is our normal waking self, while the subliminal self approximates to what we

[1] Recently, Mrs Willett (Mrs Coombe-Tennant) has reappeared as a post-mortem communicator in the automatic scripts of another medium, Geraldine Cummins. See G. Cummins, *Swan on a Black Sea*, edited by S. Toksvig with a foreword by C. D. Broad (Routledge, London 1965).

now term the unconscious. The term subliminal derives from the writings of the mortal Frederick Myers, who was one of those who anticipated Freud by giving attention to unconscious processes. However, Myers's concept seems to have differed in some important ways from Freud's, seeming closer to present day work on ASCS. Myers was more positive about the unconscious, regarding it 'as a gold mine as well as a rubbish heap', whereas Freud was more concerned with the polluting effects of the garbage; of repressed desires threatening rationality. By a gold mine Myers meant that he regarded the unconscious as a source of creativity and genius. Further, rather than writing of the unconscious as if it were an entity, Myers wrote of dissociated conscious states; of streams of consciousness which function in dreams, hypnosis, creativity and multiple personality.

The transcendental self is a fundamental concept in both Yogic philosophy and the philosophy of Kant. It is the supposed inner universal self beyond the social self, the centre of experiencing. Following death, the 'Myers' and 'Gurney' controls stated, the mind becomes dyadic instead of triadic and consciousness combines with the unconscious. This leaves the transcendental consciousness separate and it is this which they claim functions in telepathic communication.

Now, whether we dismiss this as dramatisation of an earthly subconscious mind or not, three points seem important. First, this post-mortem philosophy shows some degree of consistency as expressed through the different channels of Mrs Leonard and Mrs Willett. This is difficult to explain since neither was interested in philosophy nor had a deep knowledge of it. Secondly, the philosophy seems to be more than a reflection of that in current vogue, especially in its use of transcendental concepts. Finally, I find it fascinating that these descriptions tally with the experience of many subjects during ASC. This is especially true of those reported in the LSD literature, which often describes its own experience as reaching transcendental levels. We shall return to this later after we have seen the relationship of mediumship to other altered states of awareness.

Mediumship and other ASCs

For this we need to introduce the late Eileen Garrett, a third medium who has been studied scientifically. Again atypical of the public image of mediums, Mrs Garrett was as curious as anyone to know the meaning of her mediumship and she actively encouraged its scientific study, being responsible for the setting up of the Parapsychology Foundation from which parapsychology has received much of its financial backing. Although Mrs Garrett was never studied in the same way as Mrs Leonard and Mrs Piper (partly because by the 1930s, following Rhine, parapsychology developed techniques for studying ESP in ordinary subjects), there are some incidents to support her claims to psi experiences. One of these concerned the crash of the airship R101 in 1930, its commander appearing as a trance control and giving information about the crash that was apparently only known to a few officials. She was also assessed on the conventional ESP guessing tests by both Rhine and Soal, and Rhine found her performance in waking and trance states to be about equal, both being heavily in excess of what could be accounted for by chance. At one testing she obtained an average of thirteen hits over a series of twenty-five runs (where chance expectation was five hits per run). Yet when tested by Soal, she obtained only chance results. Before knowing this, she commented that 'the conditions at Duke are tense and emotional in comparison with those with Mr Soal in London' (Goldney and Soal 1938). This may point again to the importance of interpersonal influences in ESP and ASC research. Mediums in general have often stressed that there are bad sitters as well as good ones.

Mrs Garrett is particularly relevant to the present context because she was quite articulate about her experiences during trance, and she also experimented with other ASCs including hypnosis and LSD. In addition to this, she permitted physiological comparisons to be made between her waking and trance states. Unfortunately they revealed few obvious discernible differences (Goldney 1938) and, likewise, the EEG showed

71

only minor changes (Evans and Osborn 1952). The absence of a physiological correlate gives substance to Mrs Garrett's own belief that her trance was auto-hypnosis (since there is no known physiological correlate of hypnosis either). She describes her experiences as 'mystical union with an inner self', that she 'will yawn the conscious mind out of existence and begin to operate on another level'. At this level she felt able to reach areas of personality or mind with which she was previously unfamiliar. Certainly, auto-hypnosis as described by some exponents (G. Luthe 1972) seems to occupy a position midway between meditation and hypnosis, and is claimed to have therapeutic benefits. Hypnosis itself, according to Mrs Garrett, produced a similar but more alert state in which consciousness was more restricted (Garrett 1958). On the other hand, LSD seemed to produce a more expansive state in which she became totally absorbed in the experience and lost any sense of detachment yet at the same time felt 'completely at home with the LSD experience'. Again, this seems to indicate that trance mediumship can merge with other states of consciousness.

But what validity or meaning can be attached to these experiences? As a scientist, I am taught to reject them as more anecdotes devoid of any hard core of experimentation, and as a trained clinician, I am inclined to discount, or at most re-interpret, them as representing contact with 'repressed experiences', 'split-off parts of the self', or 'regressed childhood fantasies'. Yet common sense says there is more to it than this. Perhaps, rather than attempting to translate these experiences into objective terms or strip them of their meaning, we need to accept them as experientially valid and develop concepts specific to the state of consciousness with which we are dealing, as has been suggested by others (Tart 1971, Rao 1973). This does not mean giving up the scientific method, but we may need to re-define reality relative to our state of consciousness or brain processes.

I feel that an explanation is needed for the absence of more 'objective' experiments in mediumship literature, as well as for the antiquity of some of the investigations reported in this chapter. While a major part of the research on altered states of consciousness has been done in the last five years, most of the research on mediumship is fifty years old. This is because most mediums prefer to work with real life situations (free response material) rather than with the more formal guessing tests of ESP. It took several decades for the evolution of satisfactory techniques to assess free response material, by which time there were few good mediums around. In the 1930s, for example, Mrs Garrett was given some tests by Gaither Pratt at Duke University. The procedure involved getting the medium's clients to rate how probable it was that Mrs Garrett's statements applied to them. Unfortunately, many of the statements were not independent of each other and this created problems. Guessing correctly that someone was a man, for example, a lot of other things might follow. Recently Pratt and Birge devised a method to overcome this, using groups of 'target persons' attending anonymously in the next room. The medium's statements about the target persons can be divided into separate items which can in turn be rated for appropriateness and then compared with chance expectation (Pratt 1969). More sophisticated refinements of this have been developed since (Roll and Burdick 1969), including the use of an identikit with which the medium can make up a picture of the target person (Roll 1971).

As yet, results from these methods have been inconclusive, probably because of the scarcity of good mediums. But some 'sensitives', as they now prefer to be called, have recently produced good evidence of ESP on guessing tests. Michael Bessant, an English sensitive, after succeeding in precognitive dream studies (Chapter Four), also demonstrated his ability in a formal testing situation in which the guesses and targets were automatically recorded.

Other than these experiments, mediumship as a phenomenon seems to be largely historical. This does not, however, seem a good reason for ignoring it as much of the research seems to have been carried out with a high degree of competence.

Indeed, indulgence in certain types of ASCs appears to go through fashions, and we would have as little justification for dismissing the authenticated accounts of mediumship as our descendants would for dismissing all psychedelic experiences as invalid because some of them have had a bad press.

4
Dream States and ESP

Each night we spend about eight hours in several altered states of consciousness, but for most of us, sleep is merely an inconvenient if necessary period in which we replenish our energies. Even dreams tend to be remembered as unpleasant interruptions to what we regard as a totally quiescent state.

During the last fifteen years there has been a prolific increase in research on sleep and dreams. Thanks largely to the work of Joe Kamiya (1961) and David Foulkes (1962), we know now that consciousness, far from ceasing its activity during sleep, is continually active and exists in at least three distinct forms, some as intense and rich in imagery as the waking state.

Much of the research in this area followed the discovery by Nathaniel Kleitman and Eugene Aserinsky in 1953 of an objective means of indicating when dreams occur during the course of sleep. This discovery was the index of rapid eye movements (REMs) which were found to accompany dream periods. The combination of electro-oculograph (EOG) to record them and electro-encephelograph (EEG) to record the brain's electrical activity enabled researchers to awaken subjects during REM and non-REM periods and distinguish the different experiential states of sleep. As a result, the accepted negative view of dream experience has changed since it is possible by this method to obtain a much more representative sample of dreams than by having to rely on the small proportion of them which are remembered on awakening, largely because of their emotional content. By this method, 'the average dream' was found to be much more pleasant, far less bizarre and much less emotional than the impression we have of them from those we remember (Foulkes 1966). As we shall see later, a more positive view of dreams is also implied from the research on post-hypnotic and 'lucid dreams' in which a degree of conscious control over the dream experience is gained.

Probably the most significant feature of dreams is their implicit meaning. In many cultures, at various times, dreams have been accorded great reverence as having a prophetic and oracular nature. In contemporary society, largely due to the popularisation of Freud, we regard them as insightful rather than prophetic, revealing something about the past rather than the future. But the research evidence suggests that dreams may indeed have some prophetic potential, and that both views are probably partial truths in what is now recognised to be a complex and multiphasic process. Such research is based on collections of 'spontaneous' material and on the experimental awakenings from REM periods.

Spontaneous ESP in dreams

A fairly typical example of an apparent precognitive (prophetic) dream was reported by Mark Twain. In their youth, he and his brother worked on a Mississippi river boat and one night he awoke from a dream in which he had seen his brother's corpse lying in a metallic coffin supported by two chairs. On his chest was a bouquet of flowers with a crimson bloom in the middle. The experience was so impressive that he awoke believing his brother lay dead in the next room. In reality, it was a few weeks later that his brother, separated from him, was mortally injured when the boilers of the boat in which he was returning blew up. Most of the victims were buried in wooden coffins but he had been befriended by some ladies who had taken pity on him, and donated towards a metal coffin. When Mark Twain arrived, the scene was exactly as he had dreamt, except for the flowers. While he stood there, a lady entered carrying a bouquet of white flowers with a red rose in the centre and placed them on the corpse (Stevenson 1970).

Whether such experiences are valid instances of what they seem to be—precognitions of future events—dreams are the state of consciousness in which spontaneous ESP is most frequently reported. Louisa Rhine (1962) found that they accounted for 65 per cent of all cases reported to her. They also contained the greatest amount of complete information about the event. Thus 91 per cent of 'realistic dreams' contained complete information as compared to 49 per cent of waking experiences. Conviction, however, is not so great with dreams, possibly because they can be discounted along with other dreams as irrational, while waking ESP experiences—in the form of hallucinations, for example—force their attention directly upon normal consciousness.

Louisa Rhine (1955) also looked into the paradox implicit in precognition: if future events can be foretold, does this imply a fatalism in which the event is unavoidable; if not, how can it be foretold? Of the 191 cases in which intervention has been attempted, Louisa Rhine found that 131 were successful. However, when she eliminated cases in which some other explanation could have been responsible—normal or paranormal in the case of telepathy or clairvoyance—there were only nine cases left in which there appeared to be no doubt that the action did change the course of events, and that this action would not have occurred without the warning. Perhaps in these cases, free will lies in the use of precognitive knowledge to alter the event.

Obviously, a major fallacy with spontaneous material is that most of the cases may be spurious rather than genuine and therefore any features extracted may not be representative of the genuine cases. It is always open to the sceptic to argue against there being any genuine cases at all. Considering the number of dreams we have, it is to be expected that a few come true, and these of course may be selectively remembered. Moreover, precognitions invariably concern likely events—political assassinations, deaths, disasters. Again, only experimentation can decide the issue.

Despite this there are some spontaneous cases which seem

impressive. Ian Stevenson, psychiatrist and parapsychologist at the University of Virginia, has collected ten cases of apparent precognition of the sinking of the *Titanic* (Stevenson 1960). J. C. Barker, an English psychiatrist, collected thirty-five cases concerning the Aberfan disaster. In twenty-four of these there was corroboration that the percipient had spoken of his experience beforehand, and most of the cases were dreams. In one case, one of the children was alleged to have foretold her death on the morning of the disaster (Barker 1967).

W. E. Cox had the ingenious idea of comparing the number of passengers who were on trains involved in serious accidents with the number present on corresponding days during the weeks before the accident. He discovered that the number of passengers was much smaller on the day of the accident and the effect was most pronounced for Pullman passengers who would have to cancel their reserved tickets (Cox 1956).

Although spontaneous cases by their nature can always be explained without recourse to paranormal concepts by some hitherto overlooked factor—or, in the last resort, coincidence—they do seem to form distinctive types of experiences. This is particularly true of precognitive dreams which seem more emotional, vivid and realistic than ordinary dreams (Stevenson 1970, Louisa Rhine 1966). However, they reflect the same influence of past associations, personal interests and motives as do ordinary dreams.

Precognitive dreams seem rare occurrences. Despite this, J. W. Dunne claimed to have frequent precognitive or premonitory dreams and wrote *An Experiment with Time*, a book in which he suggested that the keeping of a dream diary would show a high incidence of fulfilment. Later attempts by others (Besterman 1933, Hart 1959) failed to confirm this. Hornell Hart optimistically estimated that only 3 per cent of dreams are strongly suggestive of precognition. There is the additional problem that precognitions can be self fulfilling in the sense that they express our unconscious or unaccepted desires rather than a paranormal experience. It seems likely that if future events have an effect on dream consciousness, it is only an occasional one, but the same may not be true of telepathic effects, as we shall see later from the experimental findings.

We now turn to the main determining influence on dream content, that of past associations. It is to Freud that credit must go in showing that dreams are meaningful events.

The meaning of dream content

Although there have been attempts to regard dreams as side products or epiphenomena of biochemical processes, these have failed to account for the meaningful nature of the dream and its attribute of consciousness. Even the original psychoanalytic theory (Freud 1954) was deficient in this respect, in that it was couched in terms of analogies with concepts drawn from the physical sciences of the time rather than in terms of experiences and processes.

Freud regarded dreams as 'the royal road to the unconscious', in the belief that they expressed the language and content of the unconscious and its wish-fulfilment of repressed desires. Thus, the dream process achieves gratification of repressed impulses by avoiding both the moral censorship of the 'superego' and the critical evaluation of the 'ego' by the use of symbolisms and displacements. The material of the dream derives from memories of recent activities, especially of the previous day, which Freud called 'day residues'. These in turn trigger off infantile conflicts and impulses that gain expression through the dream's symbolic processes.

For Freud, dreaming is an altered state of consciousness because it is necessary for consciousness to function in this way for the fulfilment of repressed desires. It is therefore a much more primitive form of experiencing in terms of analogies, concrete symbols and visceral sensations, compared with the logical and cause-effect thinking of waking consciousness. Freud uses this as evidence for an anthropomorphic 'unconscious' lurking in the background and responsible for the formation of the dream, which 'is like a firework which takes hours to prepare but goes off in a moment' (quoted in Foulkes 1964).

Yet the existence of different states of consciousness need not be interpreted as evidence for the unconscious, since, as William James once argued, it may just be an intrinsic property of consciousness itself to exist in different forms. A more modern variation of this view is that put forward by David Foulkes. On the basis of experimental evidence he concludes that 'we seem to dream as physiological recycling indicates, not as a relative degree of latent psychological trauma dictates' (Foulkes 1964). As we shall see later, the experimental evidence suggests that while there is a pre-dream period during which the transformation of day-experiences into a dynamic form seems to occur, mental activity is continuous, with no preparatory period of 'unconscious' activity. Moreover, the time spent in dreaming is very much constant and does not appear to vary according to the neurotic state of the person or his number of repressed desires. It seems more likely that emotional and dynamic problems utilise the pre-existing state of consciousness rather than determine it.

Other critics have attacked Freudian dream theory over its symbolism. Why should sex be symbolic in one dream and blatant in another? Why should a person dream of riding a horse on one night and making love to his mother on the next? Calvin Hall (1959) has suggested that different symbolisms can have different meanings. Sexual intercourse has various meanings relating to its reproductive, sensual, achievement and aggressive aspects. Hence symbols are chosen which express its personal meaning in a specific context. A snake may symbolise its evil aspects, a tower its achievement and a gun its aggressive aspect.

Hall proposed that instead of a wish fulfilment function, dreams may have a more positive purpose—that of problem solving. The dream process is a continuation of problems encountered in waking life and also an attempt at their solution, using the intuitive form of ideation in dreams. Symbols thus express the problem at a more concrete, emotive level and the solution is evolved through the use of symbolic analogies and associations. Consequently, dreams are not merely an expression of neurotic problems but an attempt at 'working through' them. On this basis it is easy to understand how problems which are not solved by logical processes will often receive a solution in dreams and how many creative discoveries can be attributed to the dream consciousness (Chapter One).

Certainly, Hall's theory is more consistent with what we know about dream processes from their experimental study using the EOG-EEG technique.

The experimental study of dream processes

When William Dement and Nathaniel Kleitman (1957) at the University of Chicago replicated the original work on eye movements during sleep, they found that 80 per cent of their cases reported experience of a dream when awakened from an REM period. Furthermore, the estimated length of the dream corresponded closely to the length of the REM period. Ralph Berger and Ian Oswald (1962) at the University of Edinburgh, found that active rather than passive dream roles were associated with periods of REMs. The conclusion (later doubted by Oswald) was that eye movements during sleep monitor imagery in the same way that they do in waking life.

Other distinct physiological and experiential stages of sleep have been identified. During the non-REM (NREM) periods investigators tried asking for 'feelings', 'thoughts' or 'emotions' rather than dreams. They discovered that this criterion produced a much higher amount of recall than Dement and Kleitman had found (Foulkes 1962). When a criterion of 'non specific content' was used there was an insignificant difference between the percentage of recall from an REM and a NREM period (both being about 90 per cent). Recall did not depend on whether or not there was a previous REM period, so it could not be a memory of dream. As we shall see later, experience during this period tends to differ qualitatively from that of dreams in being more a period of 'thought' than of visual imagery.

The pattern of changes in mental and physiological activity as sleep proceeds has also been delineated. There are several phases of sleep defined partly by the type of brain rhythm in cycles per second (cps). In a state of drowsiness there is a decrease in the rapidity of eye movements which accompany imagination and an increase in the presence of the alpha rhythm (ten to fourteen cps) recorded by the EEG. With the onset of sleep a hypnogogic period of vivid hallucination is usually reported, during which there are slow eye movements and predominant alpha activity. This develops into the first stage of sleep, 'stage one descending', as the eye movements cease and alpha becomes interspersed with theta (four to six cps) waves. In stage two there is a further lowering of voltage waves, delta (one to three cps) and spindle-shaped waves becoming frequent. The remaining stages three and four are arbitrarily defined by a further increase in delta activity. All these stages are periods of NREM during which subjective experience is one of 'thought dreams'.

It is the next stage 'ascending stage one' in which REMs and hallucinatory dreams are reported, and it is so called because dreaming in some aspects entails a shift towards a lighter depth of sleep. With the visual imagery there is a return to a predominance of alpha rhythm.

Ascending stage one occurs after sixty to ninety minutes of NREM periods and lasts between ten and sixty minutes, increasing in duration as sleep progresses. Consequently, sleep consists of repeated cycles of the order: stages one, two, three, four, three, two and one. One night may include four of these cycles with four or five REM periods. This culminates in about two hours of dreaming and six hours of 'thought dreams'.

Experientially then, sleep includes three main ASCs; the hypnogogic sleep-onset, the 'thought-dream period' and the dream state.

The hypnogogic state
This is the period between sleep and waking characterised by vivid hallucinations, slow eye movements and the presence of alpha rhythm. Some specific experiences are reported in 95 per cent of awakenings, and these experiences differ from dreams

in that they are primarily visual and lack emotional content (Foulkes and Vogel 1965).

Alan Vogel, David Foulkes and Harry Trosman (1966) have classified the hypnogogic period into several ego states according to the ego's degree of control over the direction of thought and contact with reality:

1 An Intact Ego State in which there is little impairment of the ego's function.

2 A Destructuralised Ego State corresponding to 'descending stage one', during which reality contact becomes impaired and thought is 'regressive' with bizarre, irrational, acausal images.

3 A Restructuralised Ego State corresponding to 'descending stage two', and here the thought content is more plausible, realistic and less regressive. Contact with reality has, however, been lost.

Because these states are relatively independent of physiological measures, Vogel *et al.* proposed a psychodynamic explanation to account for the sequence. They suggested that the loss of external stimulation reduces the ego's logical (secondary process) thought so that stimulation now comes from within (primary process). With the consequent loss of contact with reality, the ego attempts to regain its control over thought processes and the NREM thought dream results from this.

Although it is a philosophical point, I find it interesting that such expositions have to credit the ego with some kind of unity or continued existence behind the changing landscape of consciousness. I would speculate that the frequent occurrence of out-of-the-body experiences during the hypnogogic period may be related to this rapid change in consciousness relative to the ego. Considering the 'shift in state' hypothesis, there is evidence that ESP is facilitated by such rapid changes. If this occurs during a state in which logical processes are retained but reality orientation lost, it would explain how such experiences are interpreted as out-of-the-body experience since reality is viewed from the locus of the ESP impression.

The NREM thought period

Reports of the NREM period of sleep indicate that consciousness here is absorbed in thought with less elaborate associations and imagery than during the REM dream. It typically lacks the hallucinations and perceptual content of dreams and most of the thought is focused on reminiscences of recent events (Foulkes 1966). The difference from ordinary REM dreams is so great that judges are able to distinguish between reports from NREM and REM periods at a 90 per cent level of accuracy (Monroe, Rechtschaffen, Foulkes, Jensen 1965).

This NREM period probably has a vital function since subjects taking part in sleep deprivation experiments show an enormous rebound of NREM periods during their recovery. Allan Rechtschaffen and co-workers (1963) at the University of Chicago have produced evidence that a major function of NREM periods might be to work over the 'day residues' of recent experiences and transform them into a more dynamic (Freudian) representation to reappear during the REM dream period. Themes appearing in the NREM period often do reappear in a dramatised form in the REM period.

Thus the NREM consciousness may perform the function which Freud attributed to the unconscious, dramatising and transforming the content of recent events into a dynamic and emotional presentation.

The REM dream state

This has been called paradoxical sleep because, while there are many features which suggest it is a light depth of sleep, there are other aspects which contradict this. Heart rate, blood pressure, respiration rate, all increase with its onset, indicating arousal. However, it is more difficult to awaken subjects from it and to evoke a physiological response from the cortex of the brain.

This contradiction may be resolved by supposing that attention is dominated by the internal imagery and the body is aroused in relation to this. Just how dominant is the effect of internal imagery on consciousness is shown by the relative failure of attempts to incorporate external stimuli into dreams. Even bombarding unfortunate subjects with water sprays and flashing lights had only a moderate effect on dream content (Dement and Wolpert 1958). Ralph Berger tried instead to introduce more meaningful stimuli, such as the names of girl or boy friends, into dreams. This had an effect on dream content in about 50 per cent of the cases, the name often becoming disguised by assonance—Sheila, for example, became Schiller—and woven into the context of the dream (Berger 1963).

Further evidence for the psychological function of dreams comes from the dream deprivation experiments of William Dement. Dement used the EEG-EOG technique to awaken his subjects and deprive them of about 70 per cent of their REM (dream) periods. He noticed three main effects: progressive increase in the amount of REMs with increase in the period of deprivation, a rebound effect in the amount of REM after deprivation was over, and detrimental personality effects such as anxiety and difficulty in concentration. He concluded that there is 'a need to dream' which is consistent with Freudian theory (Dement 1960). However, there has been difficulty in repeating these experiments and in Dement's own replication the REMs increased so much that the drug dextredine had to be used to suppress their appearance, possibly resulting in a side effect on behaviour. If there is an effect on behaviour, there are probably large individual differences. Of Dement's subjects, one was deprived of eight nights REM and showed no change, and two others were deprived of sixteen nights, one becoming impulsive and the other paranoid!

Some further evidence for a psychodynamic view of dreaming is the finding by Rechtschaffen and Foulkes that the emotionality and vividness of dreams are related to indices of psychological disturbance, from which they inferred that dreams may discharge the conflicts and tensions of waking experience (Foulkes 1966).

On the other hand, authorities such as the well-known French physiologist Michel Jouvet have taken an opposing view of dreams—that the REM period, rather than serving a wish-fulfilment or problem-solving function, may represent a physiological period during which important biochemical changes occur, and so it could be argued that the need to dream is purely physiological.

The neurophysiology of sleep

The main area of the brain which has been implicated in sleep is the reticular activating system consisting of parts of the brain stem known as the Pons and the Medulla, as well as part of the mid-brain region called the Thalamus. G. Morruzi and H. Magoun had found that electrical stimulation of these areas produced waking while their destruction resulted in coma. F. Bremer found that severing above the Pons and Medulla produced characteristics of waking in animals, while severing below it resulted in permanent sleep. The conclusion was that the sleep centre lay in the Pons.

Jouvet studied the substructures of the Pons involved in the sleeping and waking behaviour of cats. One of these is the raphe nuclei which is rich in serotonin (a chemical which seems to have an inhibitory effect on transmission between nerve synapses and was at one time supposed to be the agent behind schizophrenic and psychedelic experiences). In this context, serotonin is important because it may produce monoamine toxins, and since destruction of the raphe nuclei produces permanent wakefulness, a biochemical theory in which REM periods are responsible for the dissipation of these monoamines was proposed by Jouvet (1967a, b).

Another dense collection of neurons in the Pons, the coerulus nuclei, is rich in monoamino oxidase which is responsible for the breakdown or catabolism of monoamines, and since inhibitors of monoamine oxidase result in suppression of REMs, it follows that this system might promote REM sleep (Jouvet 1967a).

Other rival systems have been proposed. The great Mexican physiologist, Paul Hernandez Péon, produced research in favour of the hypothalamus being a sleep centre since stimulation of its pre-optic area promotes NREM sleep.

One outcome of physiological research is to suggest that the original Freudian thesis of dreams expressing repressed sexual desires may have been misconceived due to a neurological co-incidence. The hypothalamus, as well as being a sleep centre, is one of the main homeostatic regulators for hormonally controlled behaviour such as sexual activity. Thus it could be maintained that sexual arousal during sleep and dreams is a side effect of hypothalamus activity.

But the matter has become complex, and the number of nominations for sleep systems multiplies each year (between 1960 and 1966 the number increased from two to six), so that 'sceptics might suggest all regions of the brain interact in producing sleeping and waking' (Thompson 1966).

Although findings on the physiology of sleep are anomalous, they do question the role of ASCs during sleep. To me the studies reviewed previously make it unlikely that they are 'epiphenomena'. Foulkes (1966) has tried to reconcile physiology with psychology by conceding that while physiological factors may be responsible for the occurrence of dreaming, once initiated, the content of the dream period is determined by psychodynamic factors such as those suggested by Freud and Hall.

We now turn to the influence of paranormal factors on dream content. Freud, as well as being an exponent of the influence of repressed sexual and aggressive drives on the content of dreams, also drew attention to their possible telepathic influence in the therapeutic situation. This position has been maintained by many later analysts (Devereaux 1953). Recently it has also been subjected to scientific evaluation using the same technique of EEG-EOG awakenings which proved so successful in the study of their psychodynamic content.

The parapsychology of dreams

If Freud was the first to attach scientific importance to ESP in dreams, the credit for being the first to devise a method to test for it experimentally must go to the Maimonides Dream Laboratory team in New York. The method they used was ingenious and simple, incorporating several of the features of the real-life phenomenon into the laboratory situation. As a radical departure from the repetitious Zener card guessing tests, they used reproductions of famous art pictures as targets. Since these often have an emotional content they are obviously more suited as a stimulus to be incorporated into dreams. The agent, who is located in a separate room or separate building from the subject, concentrates on one of these pictures chosen at random from a large pool of cards. The subject's dreams are then monitored, using the electrophysiological recording of the EOG-EEG technique in order to awaken him after each dream period and obtain a tape recording of his dream. At the completion of the experiment, the set of dream records and target pictures are presented in random order to the subjects or to judges who are asked to match the two sets, and the correspondence is compared statistically with what could have arisen by chance.

Later experiments kept to the same methodology but, in a further effort to simulate real-life experiences, the target material was both diversified and intensified. Efforts in this direction included having the agent 'act out' randomly chosen themes (Ullman and Krippner 1969), placing him in an audio-visual chamber (Krippner *et al.* 1971). For example, if the agent was given a target picture depicting an artist it would be accompanied by canvas and paints so that he could act out the role of being the artist. In the audio-visual chamber the agent would be shown a sequence of coloured slides and sound effects structured around a particular theme such as '2001', 'Police' or 'Birds'.

In 1971 the Maimonides team moved from investigating telepathic dreams to precognitive dreams, using as a subject an English sensitive, Malcolm Bessant, who had a previous history of precognitive experience. As in previous experiments the subject was awakened after each REM period and a dream account elicited, but in this case he attempted to dream about 'a special waking experience' to which he would be exposed the next day. The theme for this was chosen in the morning from a catalogue of dream items, and their frequency produced by Calvin Hall and then elaborated as a multi-sensory experience using various auditory, gustatory, tactile and visual sensations. Judges were asked to match the dream records to descriptions of these special waking experiences presented in random order. They were able to do so at a statistically highly significant level (Krippner, Ullman and Honorton 1971). A replication was likewise successful at a similar level of significance (Krippner, Honorton and Ullman 1972).

In all, between 1966 and 1972 the Maimonides team completed twelve studies using that methodology (Honorton 1973).[1] The breakdown of their results reveals a consistency almost unparalleled anywhere in parapsychology. Of the twelve projects, nine yielded statistical deviations in favour of the ESP hypothesis often at a high level of significance. Six of the studies were replications of some sort and three of these were successful (Ullman and Krippner 1969, Krippner and Ullman 1970, Krippner, Honorton and Ullman 1972).

In evaluation, the only fair criticism seems to be that their early work used a large number of analyses which may have allowed significances to arise by chance, but this would not account for the continued consistency. Certainly the usual counter-ESP explanations, such as sensory leakage, subliminal cues or failure to publish the non-significant experiments (or 'failures'), did not apply here. As with hypnosis it might be claimed that the results are due to 'luck' in discovering a few highly selected ESP subjects rather than the technique itself. This could be a factor since most of the projects involved three subjects, one of whom was selected from a group of twelve, another was discovered at a previous laboratory and a third was the known sensitive, Malcolmss Beant, but this would not account for the later successes with groups of subjects (Krippner *et al.* 1971, Honorton, Krippner and Ullman 1972).

The main problem with the Maimonides experiments does

[1] For a more popular account of this work see M. Ullman, S. Krippner and A. Vaughan, *Dream Telepathy* (Macmillan New York 1973; Turnstone Books, London 1973).

not concern the validity of their evidence for ESP in dreams, but concerns the usual problem in parapsychology of 'reproducability'. How repeatable are their findings by other laboratories? To date there are only four reported attempts to repeat their findings, two of which are methodologically weak. One, by Gordon Globus in 1968, used a similar method but included hypnogogic fantasy in the dream material and a consensus matching of targets to dreams by judges. This yielded nonsignificant results, but unfortunately the judges differed widely in confidence over their ratings and matchings. The pilot series by Calvin Hall (1967) produced some evidence of telepathy, but Hall's experiment did not guard against normal sensory communication as well as did the Maimonides experiments, and arbitrarily selected data were offered as evidence.

Hall's successful subject was Robert Van de Castle, a clinical psychologist well known for his research on sleep, who also took part in the replication attempted by Edward Belvedere and David Foulkes (1971). This was an attempt to repeat an earlier and highly successful study by Stanley Krippner and Montague Ullman (1970) in which Van de Castle had again been the subject. This was a standard type experiment involving the matching of dream reports to targets; Belvedere and Foulkes in their pilot series used the same method without success.

This might seem to be the demise of all hopes of repeating results in parapsychology, when not only the same method but the same subject fails to reproduce results twice obtained by other experimenters. But a close examination of the Belvedere and Foulkes report reveals some important differences. Van de Castle noticed at Maimonides that there was a much greater atmosphere of belief in ESP and he felt that 'the red carpet was rolled out'. At Foulkes's Wyoming laboratory there was less confidence and the experimenters were more pressed for time.

Another difference which may be important, in the light of what we know about interpersonal and relationship factors, was in the selection of agents. At the Maimonides Laboratory, Van de Castle was allowed to choose his agents from 'any member of staff he desired to serve as an agent'. At Wyoming, apparently, he was given less freedom and had to choose two out of three.

Undaunted by their initial lack of success, Foulkes and Belvedere made a second attempt to repeat the Maimonides findings (Foulkes, Belvedere, Masters, Housten, Krippner, Honorton, Ullman 1972), and this time they attempted to repeat a study that the Maimonides team had made jointly with the distinguished researchers R. E. L. Masters and Jean Housten of the Foundation for Mind Research. This was the study in which the agent had undergone 'sensory bombardment' in an audio-visual chamber located in Masters and Housten's laboratory. The agent saw slides and sound effects relating to a randomly chosen theme such as a birth of a baby, and tried to affect the subjects' dreams by this (Krippner *et al.* 1971).

In Foulkes and Belevedere's attempt at replication, all three teams (Wyoming, Maimonides and the Foundation for Mind Research) collaborated, but this time, alas, when the agent was located in Foulkes's laboratory, the results were non-significant. While agreeing that the findings did not detract from the validity of the Maimonides claims, Foulkes *et al.* concluded: 'The Maimonides studies are not free of the inter-laboratory and inter-investigator problems of replicability which have plagued other areas of parapsychological research.'

Allan Rechtschaffen, a colleague of Foulkes at the University of Chicago and distinguished for the research mentioned previously on dream states, has been more fortunate with his work on ESP in dream states (Rechtschaffen 1970), although this also seemed to implicate an experimenter factor. Rechtschaffen began some informal investigations with the question: 'What happens if both agent and subject are in an ASC during an ESP experiment—if one dreamer signals to another?' He used several methods to investigate this and with each he had remarkable success in the initial sessions while later sessions were not so successful.

The first method attempted to introduce an external stimulus into one subject's dreams and observe its effects on the dreams of the other, but, as we noted previously (page eighty-five), it is very difficult to affect dream content this way. Despite the ineffectiveness of the stimulus, however, the dreams of the two subjects seemed to correspond.

The first subject dreamt he was at a party surrounded by his brothers and sisters who were casually dressed and eating pizza. In the background Otis Redding's 'Dock of the Bay' was playing and the subject thought of his death in a crash.

The other subject dreamt he was at a celebration (party?) with fraternity brothers and sisters (brothers and sisters?) dressed in jeans and T shirts (casually dressed?). They went to a restaurant in a lake area (pizza, 'Dock of the Bay'?) where a band was playing. Some children were playing and he was worried there might be a crash and there almost was.

Rechtschaffen's second method made use of the influence of post-hypnotic suggestion on dream content (Tart 1966). The initial series seemed again to be highly successful.

The first subject was given a post-hypnotic suggestion to dream of Martin Luther King and the fear of riots. In accordance with the suggestion he dreamt that Martin Luther King had been shot; a rock was thrown and they feared a riot.

The other subject (who did not receive any suggestions) dreamt of a negro policeman beating another man and he was afraid that someone would throw a brick and start a riot.

(Apparently, these were the only dreams produced for matching.)

Next, Rechtschaffen attempted to see what influence the hypnotic dreams (in which subjects were given suggestions to dream while in hypnosis) of one subject had on those of another. Once again there appeared to be instant success. One fortunate subject was given the somewhat idyllic suggestion to dream that 'You fall in love with a beautiful girl in the Spring'. He dreamt in accordance with the suggestion 'I was with a beautiful girl on a beautiful day with the sun out. . . .' The second subject, who received no instructions, likewise dreamt 'I was in a swan-like boat on a lake and I saw a really beautiful girl. The boat went over to where she was and we sat down on the ground and ate lunch.'

Since this was an informal pilot series, explanations other than ESP could not be entirely eliminated. Collusion among subjects or chance coincidences—it may be common to dream of parties, race riots and beautiful girls—could always be invoked as explanations, but Rechtschaffen was intrigued as to why success should come with the first attempt at each new technique. Naturally it is open to the sceptic to argue that there is greater room for error in the first attempts, but I would guess that the explanation has something to do with factors we have seen to be operative in hypnosis (Chapter Two) and, in a limited sense, mediumship. These are variously described as 'demand characteristics' (Orne 1959), 'experimenter expect-ancies' (Rosenthal 1966) and 'antecedent variables' (Barber 1969) of the experiment.

In this case a new experiment, compared with a replication of a previous one, probably produces much greater involvement and enthusiasm on the part of both experimenter and subject and this may explain the different results. In a discussion with Rechtschaffen, Stanley Krippner of the Maimonides team noted that they had experienced the same problem but resolved it by continually modifying the experiments in minor ways and ensuring a turnover of part-time staff.

Rechtschaffen's experiments also illustrate another un-fortunate hazard in parapsychology. Despite the evidence for their plausibility they failed to gain the necessary financial backing and support and were never completed. However, some work has been done on hypnotic dreams and post-hypnotic control of dreaming, which confirms that both techniques may be useful for influencing dream processes and introducing extrasensory effects.

Hypnotic dreams

Although they sometimes produce REMs (Brady and Rosner 1966), dreams during hypnosis are physiologically distinct from nocturnal dreams in that the EEG indicates that the subject is awake (Barber 1962, Tart 1964). The absence of a definite criterion to distinguish hypnotic dreams from waking imagination (REMS are also produced with imagination) has led Theodore Barber to equate the two. He criticises the view of hypnotic dreams as ASCS, suggesting that if a suitably motivated control group, matched in everything except the hypnotic procedure, was told to make up dreams, there would be little or no difference between these and the dreams of 'hypnotic subjects'. Barber describes such dreams as 'typically an unembellished imaginative product . . . banal verbal or imaginal associations to the suggested topic' (Barber 1962). But the dreams of Barber's subjects may not be 'typical'; there is evidence that hypnotic dreams also vary according to the 'demand characteristics' of the situation and the 'experimenter expectancy', so that the experimenter gets very much the sort of material he wishes. Tart (1965) and Barber (1962) have reviewed the earlier psychoanalytic work which maintained that hypnotic dreams were similar to nocturnal dreams with respect to the presence of sexual symbolism. They both concluded that it was largely due to the implicit demands of the psychoanalytic researchers that symbolic-hypnotic dreams were constructed. (An additional factor may have been the inclusion of some stage one dreams with the hypnotic dream reports from some subjects entering a nocturnal dream state.)

Tart's own work on hypnotic dreams, possibly because of the different expectancy, seemed to contradict Barber's view of these as merely 'banal verbal or imaginal associations'. In a group of *unselected* subjects, of the 70 per cent who produced dreams, 11 per cent said that they felt as if they were bodily located in a dream world and another 11 per cent described their experience as a visual hallucination, like watching a motion picture.

In analysing the data on hypnotic dreams from groups given hypnosis and imagination instructions, Tart (1966a) made the important discovery that for both groups the quality of the dreams produced depended on the depth of hypnosis experienced. Since Tart believed hypnosis can occur without a formal hypnotic induction procedure, all subjects were asked to give a 'state report' on a scale describing how hypnotised they felt (this related to objective measures of hypnotisability). This 'state report' correlated directly with the degree of vividness and realism of the dream experience; with whether or not they had thoughts, fantasies or hallucinations, or felt bodily located in a dream world.

Evidently then, hypnotic dreams are a potential means of producing rich imagery which can be directly influenced by suggestion and for this reason they have been particularly useful in the search for a reliable method of inducing ESP.

Charles Honorton and John Stump (1969), in a pilot study of hypnotically induced clairvoyant dreams, used the same type of art picture reproduction targets as were used in the Maimonides nocturnal dream studies. While in hypnosis, their subjects were given suggestions to dream about those targets which had been randomly selected and concealed in opaque envelopes. Next they were asked to match their dream descriptions to the batch of targets and were able to do so beyond chance expectation.

There have now been four successful replications or variations on this technique (Parker and Beloff 1970, Glick and Kogen 1972, Keeling 1971, Honorton 1972). Having previously obtained a successful replication of the Honorton and Stump work, John Beloff and I experienced at first hand the frustration of being unable to repeat our own results. The post-mortem on it suggested that a possible explanation lay in differences between groups of subjects. The first group of subjects were selected from personal acquaintances who were interested in the project and may have been more involved and highly motivated than the subsequent group, who were volunteers previously unknown to the experimenter. While this is obviously a *post hoc* explanation, it is in agreement with the indications of the literature previously mentioned, stressing the importance of interpersonal factors in ESP and ASC.

In an effort to isolate some of the other factors relating to the specific state of consciousness conducive to ESP, Honorton's own replication applied Barber's methodology of comparing the performance of subjects in hypnosis with a (matched) 'waking-imagination' group. The ESP scores indicated hypnosis had an effect beyond that of imagination, since the evidence of ESP came only from highly suggestible subjects given hypnosis, and not from the waking-imagination group. Subjects with a high 'dream quality' rating and high 'state reports' obtained significantly more hits than those with low scores, implying that the intensity of the ASC was an important factor for success in the ESP test. Evidence was also produced for the 'shift in state hypothesis' (Chapter One) in that subjects in the hypnosis group who reported a strong change or shift in their subjective state of awareness between the pre-hypnosis and the hypnotic dream period produced significantly more hits than those showing little change.

An important tie-up between the two sets of factors, interpersonal and subjective states, is the method mentioned earlier for influencing dream states; the use of post-hypnotic suggestions to control the content of dreams.

The effect of post-hypnotic suggestions on nocturnal dreams

As well as affecting the content of hypnotic dreams, suggestions given during hypnosis can influence the content of nocturnal dreams. In certain experiments using the EOG-EEG technique, subjects highly sensitive to hypnosis who were given suggestions to dream about a particular theme and then woken up that night showed a definite influence of the suggestions on their dream content (Tart 1966, Tart and Dick 1970). For example, Charles Tart and Lois Dick at the University of California gave their subjects suggestions during hypnosis that they would later dream about some short Krishnamurti narratives read to them. The result was that most of their subjects (eight out of thirteen) reported at least one dream in which the narrative was the dominant theme. Furthermore, the number of 'narrative elements' contained in their dreams related to the hypnotisability scores of the subjects, particularly their 'state reports' of how hypnotised they felt.

This demonstrates how suggestions given in one state of

consciousness can influence the experiences in another. In this case, the suggestion was given in the hypnotic state, but the 'expectancies' and 'demand characteristics' of the waking state may operate in a similar fashion.

Dreams, telepathy, empathy and expectancy

One of the main propositions made in Chapter One was that inter-personal factors such as expectancy and empathy between experimenter and subject are important determinants of the experience during ASCs. Success in ESP experiments may depend crucially on the interaction of these factors.

So far then, the research on dream states gives some support to this view. It has converged in showing how dreams do not arise in a vacuum but are influenced by previous experiences and their emotional loadings, particularly the experimental situation. Tart (1964) has noted how the laboratory situation can influence not only the dream content but the dream process such that on the first night in the laboratory the subject is likely to miss his first stage one period.

Yet how do we explain it when the laboratory seems to facilitate phenomena in excess of the real life equivalent? This seems to me to be the case with the Maimonides work if we discount the possibility that their results are due to a few special subjects. If a sizeable number of subjects' dreams can show a measurable extrasensory influence of what must be regarded as an unconsequential and artificial stimulus, then why do paranormal events account for such a meagre proportion of our dream life? In real life there must be so many potential experiences of vital importance to us that could gain expression.

There seem to be two possible answers. First, it is possible that ESP has a much greater effect on our dream experiences than we are aware because of the selectively few dreams we recall. Obviously, if this is a valid supposition it could constitute an important discovery.

Ostensibly, it seems more likely that success is augmented by the experimental situation. If both experimenter and subject are highly involved in the ESP task then, as stated previously,

97

it is possible that the 'demand characteristics' act upon the dream experience parallel to the way post-hypnotic suggestions were shown to operate, thereby focusing the dream consciousness on the ESP targets.

Such effects seem to be one step towards the conscious control of dreaming (Tart and Dick 1970) and there is evidence that the rich world of dream experience need not be lost to the waking consciousness.

Some individuals have been able to retain conscious awareness of the dream process while it is in operation and, in several cases, take active control over it. It is these lucid dream states and related out-of-the-body experiences that are the concern of the next chapter.

5
Out-of-the-Body Experiences and Lucid Dreams

Out-of-the-body experiences (OBEs)—in which the observer feels that his consciousness is located apart from his physical body—would be discounted as body-image disturbances belonging to the psychiatric province but for the fact that they have a high frequency amongst normal, apparently healthy individuals and, inexplicably, they do sometimes appear to be what they claim to be. Reports of the experience are estimated to come from about 20 per cent of the population (Green 1968a), and there are on record several cases where veridical information has ostensibly been acquired during such an experience (Hart 1959).

The experiences also seem to have subjective validity: 90 per cent of those who report them describe perception as real, as normal or enhanced, with their intellectual functioning unimpaired or improved (Green 1968a). They occur in a variety of circumstances; in sleep and the hypnogogic state, during stress and anxiety and fatigue. In fact, this has some consistency with what psychiatrists, using a broader category of 'depersonalisation states', have found in the normal population (e.g. Sedman 1966).

As we shall see later, while there is evidence to link OBEs (out-of-the-body experiences) to the hypnogogic or drowsiness state, many experiences also occur when the percipient is unconscious, during, say, an accident or operation. The following is an example of such a case.

As a pillion passenger on a motor bike, I was involved in a

collision with a car. I came off the back of the bike, went over my driver and over the car. Then I hit the ground, head first. I got up from the ground where I lay, surprised that I felt no pain or bruising and moved away. I saw people running and looked around to see why. Then I saw my body still lying in the road, and they were running toward that; some of them passed me as I stood there. I could hear shouts and a woman's voice crying 'She is dead!'. And then a feeling (I can still feel the awful shock of this whenever I recall the incident) of terrible fear came to me. I knew I HAD to return to my body before it was touched. There was a dreadful sense of urgency, or it would be too late. It is this sensation of dread that remains so indelible.

I went back and lay down on top of myself, and as I did so I felt the hardness of the road beneath me and all the terrible pains of bruising, lacerations and concussion that I was subsequently found to be suffering . . . I was moving about thinking I was in my normal body . . . everything looked normal . . . my 'floating self' behaved exactly as my physical. (Quoted by McCreery 1973.)

Lucid dreams fall naturally between OBEs and nocturnal dreams. In lucid dreams, the dreamer is aware that he is dreaming, can reflect on it, and sometimes take a decisive part in determining its outcome. (A prominent dream researcher has remarked how his interest in dreams stems from the period as a child when he used to have nightmares of dragons and had to invent strategies of dealing with them—first by talking to them, then by 'lopping their heads off'!) Occasionally, lucid dreams are precipitated by nightmares, perhaps as a defence against informing the self of the unreality of the situation—that 'it's only a dream'.

However, if lucid dream experience can also be accompanied by incidents of what seem to be ESP, then the distinction between this and OBEs becomes a relative one. Presence of a body image is not a distinctive factor because often a second 'spiritual' body is reported during OBEs. The main difference is that the world of OBEs approximates more to that of the waking state whereas that of the lucid dream usually contains more fantasy and symbolic elements. OBEs also seem to have a higher level of intellectual functioning and a greater intensity of feeling associated especially with what is experienced as liberation from the body.

Nevertheless, retention of memories and intellectual functioning during lucid dreams are said to improve with practice (Green 1968b). The dream reality can be so convincing that there are also cases of 'false awakenings' in which the individual believes he has awoken from his dream world when he is in fact still in it. Charles McCreery (1973) inquired: 'How then do lucid dreamers know they are dreaming?' From his case studies he concludes that there are no absolute criteria, except that 'it just feels like a dream; or the dream world he is in just has a dream-like texture'. McCreery suggests that the ultimate criterion is that if you find yourself questioning whether you are awake, it means you are asleep! An example of this is the dream of Oliver Fox (quoted by Green 1968b).

On pulling up the blind we made the amazing discovery that the row of houses opposite had vanished and in their place were bare fields. I said to my wife, 'This means I am dreaming, though everything seems so real and I feel perfectly awake. Those houses could not disappear in the night, and look at all that grass!'

We need to know much more about lucid dreams; our present knowledge is scanty. We have no idea how they relate to normal dreams and as yet there has been no report of physiological monitoring during one of these experiences. Besides their alleged paranormal content (Green 1968b), they may have some therapeutic implications. Heightened consciousness through lucid dreams compared with ordinary dreams seems to mean that a memory of the experience is retained on waking. As a result, such dreams are not lost to the waking consciousness and can provide a valuable means of self-exploration. Moreover, it has been suggested that the use of lucid dreams by the Senoi tribe (Chapter One) accounts for their relative mental and social health.

To learn more about lucid dreams, it may be feasible to develop techniques for inducing them and developing some degree of conscious control over dreaming. We noted in the previous chapter how the influence of post-hypnotic suggestions on dreams (Tart and Dick 1970, Tart 1966) might provide such a means.

Fortunately, we have more data about out-of-the-body experiences. While it is rare to have more than one OBE in a lifetime, if any, there is a small but sizeable number of people who report these experiences frequently. From the data presented by Celia Green (1968a), the number of OBEs reported in the population would seem to decrease to a certain point and then increase. Of those who have OBEs, 60 per cent report only one such experience and the percentage decreases until we reach six or more experiences, of which the estimated frequency is 20 per cent. This could be interpreted as meaning that while most people ignore (or are frightened by) them, a sizeable proportion either have some kind of innate liability to them or take an interest in cultivating the experience.

Certainly, there are many occult exponents (such as Oliver Fox, Sylvan Muldoon, P. Ouspensky, to name but a few) of 'astral projection' who claim to have developed techniques of control over these experiences. One method described by Oliver Fox was to develop his lucid dreams into OBEs. Contemporary writers who have produced fairly cogent descriptions of their OBEs include psychiatrist John Lilly, author of *The Centre of the Cyclone* (1973), and business executive Robert Monroe, author of *Journeys Out of the Body* (1971).

With so many people reporting these experiences, a reasonable question is why have they not received more formal experimental study? The reasons for this are not clear, but it was something of a breakthrough when Tart in 1967 and 1968 reported on the first laboratory studies of OBEs.

The laboratory study of OBEs

There have now been three reported OBE laboratory studies with some degree of consistency in findings (Tart 1967, 1968; Mitchell 1973). The basic method has been to monitor the experience using the same EEG-EOG technique as that for the study of dreams. In addition, the alleged extrasensory nature of the experience was tested by the placement of targets out of the range of vision.

The first investigation was a nine-session study of the OBEs of Robert Monroe conducted by Charles Tart while he was at the University of Virginia. A five-digit random number was written on a piece of paper and placed as the target on a shelf in the adjoining room. Monroe was only able to produce two OBEs during this period and reported that neither of them were stable enough to enable him to perceive the target. However, he correctly reported that at the time of the experience the technician had left her console and was in the hall talking to a man (though this is obviously open to explanations other than ESP). From the EEG record, the OBEs seemed to coincide with stage one (descending) sleep which was dominated by slowed alpha waves or alphoid rhythm.

The next investigation, a four-night study of the OBEs of a Miss 'Z', was conducted by Tart at the University of California. This subject reported three such experiences during the time and in one of them she was able to correctly identify the ESP target, again a five-digit random number. Her OBEs were accompanied by a flattened EEG record which showed prominent alphoid activity but no REMs. This also appeared to represent a stage one sleep or drowsiness (hypnogogic) period. The alphoid activity was unusual and Tart showed the records to William Dement, one of the leading authorities on sleep research, who agreed that the record was difficult to classify into any of the known sleep or drowsiness stages.

Unfortunately, as far as the ESP element was concerned, the possibility that she had subliminally perceived the target by a reflection from the clock in the room could not be eliminated. More disturbing is that Tart reports the presence of a large amount of sixty-cycle artifact during this particular OBE— and sixty-cycle artifact is what would have occurred if she had tried to move or position herself in order to see the number.

Nevertheless, these results have now received some degree of replication by Janet Mitchell and Karlis Osis of the American Society for Psychical Research. Much of this research is still in progress and has not yet been published in the scientific journals, although brief bulletins have been issued (Mitchell 1973). Their subject is the artist Ingo Swann who reports frequent OBES, often at will and retaining conscious control of his body. Mitchell's electrophysiological observations agreed with Tart's in showing that the experience was accompanied by little or no change in body physiology and a flattened EEG. But instead of a decrease in alpha *frequency* there was a decrease in the *amount* of alpha.

Some impressive evidence for the ESP content of the experience was produced by Swann. He would attempt to draw targets placed out of sight on a platform ten feet above the floor, and the drawings apparently show a remarkable degree of resemblance to the targets. Eight sets of targets and drawings were randomised and then presented to an independent judge. She correctly matched all eight pairs (which would occur by chance only once in 40,000 times).

Currently, Osis and Mitchell are attempting to discover whether the experience is a dream state conducive to ESP or whether there is an actual projection of consciousness. One test is to place the targets in an observation box which has a system of mirrors and prisms to distort the image of the targets as viewed externally. The test is to see whether the real object is perceived by direct ESP, or whether the distorted image is seen from a point in space as an observer would see it (implying a projection of consciousness as well as ESP). Tentative findings favour the latter interpretation (Osis 1973).

It would not be an understatement to say that this raises some conflict with what we know about perception. So much of the external world we see is shaped and programmed by our perceptual systems that one could not conceive of an 'eyeless vision'. Individuals who recover their sight do not perceive the stable world we call reality, but rather a blurred confusion of shapes and movements. Many months of learning are required before perception becomes an ordered compromise between the stimuli and our sensory systems. This is not say that a full explanation of perception can be made without reference to consciousness. It is one thing to explain the perception of, say, colour in terms of stimulation of the cones in the retina, chemical stimulation of neural transmission, and encoding in neural transmission to the visual cortex, but it is another to explain the *experience* of the colour as distinct from the encoding.

In fact, the OBE 'vision' of Ingo Swann would seem to differ radically from that of normal perception. It seems to be much less distinct, especially with unfamiliar shapes, and also to be sensitive to light reflections and ionisation fields. Further conclusions must await publication of more research, and this is regarded as one of the most important areas of current research in parapsychology. If OBEs are more than hallucinatory activity and are, to quote Tart, 'a dream state plus something else', then this something else may have enormous significance for psychology and philosophy.

However, there are two findings that do seem to have some reliability. These are the implication of changes in the alpha rhythm and the presence of either stage one sleep or the hypnogogic period (which overlaps with it).

Tart and Mitchell's findings on changes in alpha activity may have some support in the psychiatric literature. Most psychiatrists would subsume OBEs under the penumbra of 'depersonalisation'. This term is loosely used to include feelings of unreality, changes in body image and perception of the self. In an EEG study of seven patients experiencing 'episodic depersonalisation', K. Davison (1964) found the only unusual changes to be an excess of slower rhythms and a *slowing* of the alpha rhythm (i.e. alphoid rhythms).

The other finding, suggesting that the presence of the hypnogogic state is an important correlate of OBEs, also appears to have some consistency with other research.

The hypnogogic period

As we saw in the previous chapter on dreams, the hypnogogic period is experientially a pre-sleep stage of drowsiness with hallucinatory images. The experiential changes involve a rapid transition between three 'ego states' (which are distinguished according to the degree of intactness of reality contact and logical thought). More than at any other period, there appears to be a great deal of individual variation in these ego states (Vogel, Foulkes, Trosman 1966).

We also noticed that, physiologically, the hypnogogic period is characterised by a sequence which starts with the presence of alpha rhythm and rapid eye movements (accompanying imagination), followed by alpha with slow eye movements (hallucinations) and stage one and two sleep. These descriptions of the hypnogogic period produce a picture which is consistent with what we appear to know about ESP and OBEs, namely:

1 There is evidence to support the hypothesis that a rapid change in subjective state of awareness is associated with ESP (Honorton, Davidson, Bindler 1971, Honorton 1972a, Honorton 1972b).

2 There is evidence (which will be presented in a later chapter) to link ESP with changes in various parameters of the alpha rhythms.

3 The findings of Tart and the other researchers concur in suggesting an alphoid stage one descending as the probable physiological correlate of the out-of-the-body experience with its ostensible ESP component. This also agrees with the importance placed upon the hypnogogic period in the occult literature. (Fox 1962, Muldoon and Carrington 1956), and with the findings from the spontaneous reports (Green 1968a).

In view of this, it seems likely that OBEs are sometimes ESP experiences induced by the rapid shift in state during the hypnogogic period. Since there are tentative findings to link this specifically with the onset of stage one sleep where the ego state retains logical functions but reality contact is lost, then the experience may be one in which ESP is substituted for reality. Because logical thinking is to some extent retained, sleep consciousness may interpret this in normal spatial terms as an out-of-the-body state.

Explanations are probably premature at this stage of

knowledge but what is explained above does seem to have some empirical foundation. It must be admitted though that not all OBES occur during the hypnogogic period and the exposition explains neither the nature nor the occurrence of the ESP experience.

More research is obviously needed, and it is possible that the hypnogogic period can be utilised to induce OBES experimentally. There are methods of relaxing subjects into the hypnogogic state in the laboratory by reducing external stimulation. One of these is to send 'white noise' through the earphones worn by the subject, producing a homogeneous field at the same time by shining red light through the halves of ping-pong balls placed over his eyes. If this is combined with the technique of post-hypnotic control over dream content (Tart and Dick 1971), then it may be feasible to induce OBES by suggestion during the hypnogogic period.

'Out-of-time' experiences

Time is often perceived differently during OBES; of subjects who report more than one experience, 37 per cent report alteration in their sense of time (Green 1968a). One case of an apparent paranormal displacement in time which was linked to abnormalities in the hypnogogic period of the percipient was the Buterbaugh case, reported by the eminent psychologist Gardner Murphy, and H. L. Klemmo (1966).

Mrs Buterbaugh, secretary to the Dean of Wesleyan University, Nebraska, had been asked to deliver a message to the C. C. White building on the campus. Walking through the hallway she heard the usual sounds of students, and a marimba playing. On entering the professor's room she was suddenly repelled by a strong musty odour, the noises from the hall ceased, and looking up she saw the figure of a tall, black-haired woman dressed in early twentieth-century period clothes. The figure was reaching up to one of the shelves of the cabinet. There was also a ghostly 'presence' at the desk and, looking out of the window, the view of the campus had completely changed. Instead of the buildings and the street, there was rolling countryside. She felt she was in another time dimension, became frightened and hurried from the room back into the hall where she was immediately reassured by the familiar noises including the playing of the marimba. Mrs Buterbaugh somehow knew that the figure was unreal. 'While I was watching her she never moved. She was not transparent and yet I knew she wasn't real. While I was looking at her she just faded away—not parts of her body one at a time, but her whole body all at once.'

So far this reads like a very traditional ghost story, yet there were some interesting and inexplicable features. The detailed descriptions of the apparition fitted an old photograph, which was discovered later, of Miss Mills, a music teacher, who had died in the building shortly before 9.00 a.m. (the same time as Mrs Buterbaugh's experience), and who had worked there from 1912 to 1936. Furthermore, a 1915 photograph of the campus depicted a scene very similar to that seen by Mrs Buterbaugh out of the window; Murphy and Klemmo stated that it was very unlikely she had seen the photographs. Examination of the filing cabinet revealed choral arrangements dating back to the time of Miss Mills's tenure at the university.

Many of the details were elicited by the use of hypnosis to recover memories, which usually reveals the source of any 'unconscious' confabulations. Psychological examination of Mrs Buterbaugh suggested no mental disturbance, but she did have a history of *déjà vu* experiences, and paralysis during the hypnogogic period.

Although such cases could never constitute a proof of anything, they require explanation and it is interesting to note that Murphy and Klemmo concluded that the hypnogogic period may have been an important factor in the experience.

Apparitions and OBEs
There are a few recorded cases of out-of-the-body experiences where the apparition of the person is alleged to have been seen by others at the time of the experience. Some cases of 'travelling clairvoyance' have already been mentioned (Chapter Two).

Another example reported by the early SPR researchers is the Beard case (Gurney, Podmore, Myers 1886).

During his experience, Beard tried to make himself appear to his fiancée. Without previous warning, he 'projected' himself into her bedroom, allegedly with some effect, for his fiancée and her sister saw him and became terrified. Beard was able to repeat this on several occasions, notifying Gurney by postcard of the day of his attempt and his fiancée independently verifying his success.

Hornell Hart (1959) compared the characteristics of such apparitions of the living with those of the dead and argued that the two showed close resemblance. His interpretation was that if you can have an OBE while living, it may be possible to have one when you are dead! Whatever we may think of these cases, the early psychical researchers did give them some degree of credence.

One of the first major achievements of the SPR was the 'Census of Hallucinations'. This was a survey of the frequency of apparitions experienced in the population by people in normal health. They estimated about one in forty-three of these cases was coincidental with the death of the person hallucinated. Next, they compared this figure with the likelihood of the person dying as computed from death statistics. The result was a much higher number of 'coincidences' than the laws of chance could account for. Obviously there are flaws in using such estimates and the investigators made allowance for them, but such evidence could never be conclusive.

The most coherent theory of apparitions was put forward by G. N. M. Tyrrell (1953). Tyrrell was mainly concerned with crisis apparitions—veridical apparitions corresponding to an emotional event such as death or illness. The evidence suggested that these were hallucinations elicited by an emotional telepathic link with the person perceived. Tyrrell noted that apparitions wore clothes, responded as the person might be expected to, but left no traces. In short, they tallied with normal perception. Tyrrell compared this to a drama: the original telepathic impulse was the 'plot'; the 'producer' worked out the details and the 'stage carpenter' presented it. These personifications were meant to refer to the unconscious levels of the personality. Tyrrell viewed the self as a hierarchy of levels and degrees of 'I'ness. At deeper levels there was a relative unity of personality and the 'producers' etc. of the two persons involved could thus combine on a joint 'production' of the 'drama'. Ultimately, Tyrrell's theory has affinities with Buddhism. Apparitions have 'no heart in them' and are 'wavering, uncertain, semi-intelligent things' because, essentially, they are only an emotional, associative link between the deeper levels of individuals. This helps to remove some of the absurdities implicit in talking of localisation of OBEs, apparitions and ESP experiences in terms of physical space. Instead, the 'space' may be one of emotional or empathetic proximity.

While not wishing to take a stand over the paranormal nature of apparitional experiences—many of the cases are old and often open to alternative explanations—I have discussed them here for two reasons. First, because they have a traditional importance in parapsychology, and secondly, I believe that Tyrrell's theory may be worthy of resurrection to show how apparitions are consistent with some of the layers of the self perceived by subjects in ASCs (particularly the psychedelic and meditation states).

OBEs and other ASCs

OBEs are not specific to dream states but are reported in almost all altered states. They are frequently reported in the early research on hypnosis (Chapter Two) and in mediumship (Garrett 1934, Assailly 1963). Assailly found six out of his ten mediums had reported OBEs. Mrs Willett's consciousness, in which she received communications from the deceased 'Gurney', 'Myers' and 'Sidgwick', could best be described as a lucid dream state.

Incidents of OBEs occurring with LSD have been reported since its first synthesis and accidental use by Albert Hoffman. Describing the effects of the drug, Hoffman wrote: 'Occasionally I felt as if I were out of my body. I thought I had died. My ego seemed suspended somewhere in space from where I saw my dead body lying on the sofa' (quoted by Van Asperen de Boer *et al.* 1966). In his survey of experienced marijuana users, Tart (1971) found that 23 per cent reported having OBES. This probably does not differ from the general population, but 21 per cent had multiple experiences and most of them reported their experience to be associated with the use of either marijuana or LSD.

Recently, Lilly (1973) has written a detailed account of his exploration of 'inner space' induced by LSD and a variety of other methods. Many of his experiences show a correspondence with those described by Tart's subject Robert Monroe (1971). Lilly preferred to talk in terms of 'karmic levels'—levels of the self associated with its degree of harmony with the universe—but they both experienced 'other worlds' populated by guides, spirits, etc.

It would need little psychoanalytic expertise to dsimiss these as projections and personifications of repressed areas of the self. Yet, as we shall see later from the research on psychedelic and meditational effects, this 'repressed self' would seem to contain a multitude of experiences far in excess of the imagination of any analyst with the exception of Jung.

Psychedelic experiences and OBES such as these bear a remarkable resemblance to the experiences of the great Swedish philosopher, scientist and mystic, Emmanuel Swedenborg. Swedenborg claimed he could exist in both the world of the dead and the world of the living (or the 'inner' and 'outer' worlds). He described the spirit world as a confrontation with what we might call the person's 'id' or 'shadow'—his repressed other half. For example, the virtuous and puritanical parts were terrorised by the villainous. After this unification they passed on to higher states of consciousness (which is reminiscent of the claims made by the 'Myers' and 'Gurney' communicators in mediumship as to what occurred to consciousness following death) (Broad 1962).

Experiences of the dying

What then do people experience at death? Does it resemble an out-of-the-body experience? Karlis Osis, director of research at the American SPR, has reported an extensive survey of 'Deathbed Observations by Physicians and Nurses' (1961).

Osis sent out questionnaires to nurses and doctors concerning the experiences of the dying, and analysed the returns by computer to extract the common features. Apparently, only about 10 per cent of the dying are conscious, but amongst these the popular belief that the dying see deceased friends and relatives seems to have some validity. From his data, it would seem that about 40 per cent of his conscious, dying patients had hallucinations of relatives or friends who were in fact already dead. These occurred in clear consciousness and did not appear to relate to changes in physiology or medication. These hallucinations of recognised, deceased persons were much more frequent than those reported in corresponding surveys of hallucinations occurring in people in good health.

Visions of various scenes were also much more frequent (ten times as much) than those occurring in people in good health, but these were only experienced by people believing in life after death. To a large extent then, the Osis survey may merely confirm that when people die they see what they expect to see. Even so, one must concede it as a bit more than one would expect from the last throes of a machine ticking over.

The Osis team is currently interviewing hospital staff in India to see whether these hallucinations could be conditioned purely by cultural expectations. It would also be extremely valuable to have a survey of those who have been close to death but who have survived. Although I know of no data on this, as we saw earlier there are frequent claims of OBEs occurring during operations and accidents. One study of some slight relevance was carried out by the well-known psychiatrist Robert Lifton on the survivors of aeroplane crashes (1973). Following the accident there was sometimes a period of emotional denial and repression, but often too there was 'an increased capacity to feel the expanded consciousness that many seek in drugs or meditation'.

Towards an explanation

So far, OBEs and related phenomena seem to depict the existence of an experientially real world which sometimes appears to have extrasensory elements derived from the external world. How dependent this experiential world is on the brain we cannot say. It is possible it has its own 'space' in terms of emotions, associations, and symbolisms which may overlap with those of other individuals, such as when an apparition occurs. ESP may occur at the interface between this personal inner space and the group consensus we call reality. The ESP aspect of ASCs may imply that consciousness has its own laws and that the contradictions over OBEs arise from trying to visualise the OBES as a *physical* exteriorisation of consciousness. This is not meant to imply a phenomenalism in which only ideas exist, since such occurrences seem to cut through all the usual philosophical beliefs concerning reality. It must also be stressed that OBEs can become less dominated by personal areas and merge into other states, reaching more mystical, expansive levels.

This is obviously speculative, but it does lead to some suggestions and predictions. We need to know much more about the overlap between these 'inner spaces'. For example, we need to know if ESP can be more readily induced in individuals who are in the same ASC than in those in different states; we need to know whether experiences overlap more with two emotionally-close individuals in the same ASC than with two emotionally-remote individuals. Some preliminary work has been done (Tart 1968, Rechtschaffen 1970), but more is needed.

6
Pathological States

The view presented here is that altered states of consciousness are not necessarily healthy or pathological. They do, however, present a potential for mental growth or disturbance depending largely upon the reactions and interpretation the individual puts on the experience. This in turn is heavily influenced by the preparation and support he is given for the experience.

Many authorities would dissent from this and either dismiss ASCS as bizarre natural oddities, or maintain that they are pathological. By symptom-seeking, however, one can make a pathology out of virtually all human behaviour. For instance, if we were to apply the same criteria to being in love as those used to argue that psychedelic drugs produce psychosis, this state, with its attendant paranoia, anxiety, change in self-perception, dependency and so on, could be included as a sure sign of insanity, or any other pathology one may care to mention.

This could account for some of the success psychiatrists have in formulating an alternative view of ASCS in diagnostic terms. Almost all states have their clinical counterpart. Hypnosis has been called a 'transference neurosis', mediumship equated with secondary personality, dreams regarded as a discharge of psychotic impulses, out-of-the-body experiences subsumed under depersonalisation states, psychedelics formerly labelled psychotomimetic drugs (psychosis mimicking) and, finally, mystic states, possession, and shamanism seen as manifestations of schizophrenic processes.

At best, psychiatric diagnosis is a precarious operation. If one wanted to be unkind one could point to the notorious lack of agreement between psychiatrists in their diagnoses. In any event, meaning here can only be descriptive and would not indict any altered state by suggesting an underlying disease entity.

An example of the application of psychiatric diagnosis to ASCs is reported in a recent publication on 'Chronic Psychosis Associated with Long-Term Psychotomimetic Drug Abuse' (Glass[1] and Bowers 1970). Four case histories were presented as evidence of a psychotic state resulting from psychedelic drug usage. Their first case involved a twenty-two year old man who had shown no pathological traits until this point, and might be amusing but for its serious consequences.

He began to use marijuana occasionally at age 16 and LSD infrequently at age 18. After dropping out of his first year of college he went to San Francisco with a girl friend whom he impregnated within six months. While trying to reach a decision about marriage he began to use LSD almost daily, allegedly taking over seventy-five doses in four months. He did not marry the girl who subsequently left him and placed the child for adoption. The patient then returned home where his family found his 'hippie' appearance, his passive withdrawn manner, and his bizarre speech in sharp contrast to his previous personality. Despite the fact that he had not used any drugs except marijuana for six months the family insisted on hospitalisation because of the personality change. On admission he had shoulder-length hair, a saddened, aged face, and appeared underweight. He avoided meaningful interaction in a stereotyped manner. He would sit passively and occasionally raise his hands, saying such things as 'Don't hustle me', or 'It's a groove'. His affect was flat and bland. Word associations were not loose but revolved around a philosophical belief in eastern religions, LSD experiences, and himself as the passive agent for those things which were cosmically determined. Strong denial and projective mechanisms were apparent in his thinking although occasionally he was aware that his paranoid ideas were related to internal feelings, particularly guilt. He also experienced feelings of depersonalisation and

[1] Dr Glass has since modified his position to accept that psychedelic drugs can be therapeutically valuable if taken in a controlled supportive environment, a view with which I would concur.

visual hallucinations. Orientation was accurate and his recall for recent events was good, but recall for past events seemed vague. An electroencephalogram was read as normal. The working clinical diagnosis was chronic undifferentiated schizophrenia, and the patient was hospitalised for four months while being seen in individual and group psychotherapy. He was placed on larges doses of chloropromazine (900 mg a day) which had some calming effect but did not alter his basic manner of thinking. The passive style, preoccupation with eastern religious fatalism, and avoidance of social interaction persisted. He continued to keep his outpatient appointments and take psychotropic medication, although his mental status remained unchanged.

Undoubtedly schizophrenic reactions can occur with the illicit use of psychedelic drugs, but they are rare and, as we shall see later, the evidence suggests that they can be prevented or resolved by an empathic supportive setting. When negative reactions occur in ASCs they are probably explicable by reference to the unresolved aspects of the individual's personality dictating the experience, together with the absence of a supportive setting to help resolve them. (I am reminded here of some of the first experiments on LSD therapy by Czech researchers. If patients showed an untoward reaction to the experience, they continued with LSD sessions until it was resolved. For whatever reason they had a high therapeutic success rate!) Often the expansive consciousness associated with trance states, psychedelics and so on takes on egoistic dimensions in a 'disturbed' person, so that personal fantasies and fears become projected into the world and revered as truth. Mystical union can be solipsistic as well as pantheistic, which may account for some of the more apocalyptic religious groups having their foundations in abnormal states.

Consequently, it would seem from this that the equation of some ASCs with pathology is an over-emphasis on one end of the dimension. Recently, the argument has been turned on its head by evidence that schizophrenia can be better understood when treated as an ASC rather than a medical pathology. We shall look next at the evidence for this, and then at the 'health' versus 'pathology' dimensions of the various states of consciousness. Finally, some studies of psychotherapy will be presented which lead to two conclusions. First, that the concept of the unconscious could be better understood if it were thought of as referring to *unformed*, potential experiences and states of consciousness rather than autonomous entities. Secondly, that similar interpersonal influences operate in ensuring self-exploration of unconscious phenomena as occur in the exploration of altered states of awareness. Both creative and paranormal abilities seem to emerge during the expansion or shift in consciousness accompanying these explorations.

Schizophrenia and ASCs

The causes of schizophrenia are complex and controversial and beyond the scope of this text, but a strong case can be made for explaining schizophrenia in terms of social and family interaction. Within this ambit, a view that has recently gained support from authorities in different fields is the possibility that schizophrenia may be a natural state through which the road to self-realisation and creativity passes.

In an important publication entitled *A New Approach to Psychology: The Influence of Cultural Meanings on ASCs*, Lawrence Watson and Dixon Guthrie (1972) argue that there is a similarity between the distortions of perception experienced in pathological states and those of mysticism, LSD and shamanism. What distinguishes pathological states from healthy ones is that the experience is not voluntary, the expectations are negative, and there can be no help with the experience's interpretation from a 'guide' or 'guru'. Western society devalues or fears the irrationality of the ASC experience, and diagnosis of it as 'sick' increases the negative reaction. The main source of this cultural stress is the absence of meanings or concepts by which to interpret the experience. As Watson and Guthrie remark, 'mental disorder such as that seen in schizophrenia is therefore not only the result of an ASC and the factors which may have caused it, it is also the result of an interaction of the ASC and the available cultural meanings by which the experience is conceptualised and integrated into the life of the individual'. Societies which provide a medium for the manifestation of these states and revere their occurrence enable individuals to work through the psychotic aspects. As we might expect, such societies have either a low incidence of schizophrenia or a transient form of it.

Shamanism is an example of a state which western psychiatrists would regard as psychotic. The shaman is a Siberian medicine man, prophet and artist. The Chilean psychiatrist Claudio Naranjo has described how the shaman, during his initiation, enters a state similar to psychosis, but he is not hospitalised or treated. Instead the state is respected and allowed to take its course. With regard to schizophrenia in our own society, Ronald Laing is the most familiar supporter of this kind of approach. In a discussion of 'Transcendental Experience' (Laing 1967), he draws parallels between psychedelic and schizophrenic experiences. Both involve a journey from outer to inner and back again, culminating in existential death and rebirth. Laing suggests that during this experience the person should 'be guided with full social encouragement and sanction into inner space and time by people who have been there and back again'.

Often the evidence for a genetic or innate cause of schizophrenia is quoted as counter-evidence to this kind of approach. However, the evidence (such that it is) may only validate the existence of certain innate personality patterns which predispose the individual to certain types of ASCs; it cannot say anything about whether it is irreversible or unresolvable. There is evidence that during most ASCs the experience can move in a positive or negative direction.

Dream states
There is much evidence to suggest that those who recall their dreams are less repressed than those who shut off their dream life. 'Non-dreamers' who say they dream infrequently and, when asked to keep a record, report few dreams in their 'dream diary' have less fantasy and score higher on tests

purporting to measure repression (Schonbar 1959, Tart 1962). There is also evidence that non-dreamers score lower on ESP tests than dreamers (Honorton 1972), possibly because of the denial or lack of openness to inner experience as a whole.

It seems probable that the dream experiences of non-dreamers differ from those of dreamers. Physiologically, they appear more aroused during sleep and there is evidence that their dreams are more emotional than those of dreamers—which could explain why they forget or repress dreams. It has also been found that the vividness, distortion and emotionality of dreams relates positively to the pathological scales of the MMPI (a test designed to measure psychological disturbance). From this it seems reasonable to conclude that the intensity of dreaming, together with its denial, relates to emotional disturbance (Foulkes 1966), while recall relates to health.

The same does not seem to hold for the hypnogogic drowsiness state. Recall of dream-like fantasy from this relates negatively to measures of pathology. Together, these findings seem to imply that an involvement in dream life and integration of it with waking life is an index of health, while its dissociation from the waking state may relate to emotional disturbance.

Out-of-the-body and depersonalisation experiences

We have almost no information about how OBEs relate to mental health, although there is a large accumulation of findings on 'depersonalisation states' in both the normal and patient populations. As we noted previously, depersonalisation is used by psychiatrists to cover changes in the awareness of the self, feelings of unreality, and changes in body image. There is good reason to think that OBEs form a large proportion of these data with reference to the normal population. (I learned this to my detriment some years ago when I proposed to compare OBE's occurring in normal subjects with depersonalisation experiences in patients. The project was rejected on the grounds that there could be no differences; both belonged to the same syndrome.) It is estimated that between 40 and 50 per cent of the population report a depersonalisation experience at some time and the circumstances seem identical to ones in which OBES occur (Roberts 1960, Sedman 1966). Despite the obvious overlap between the two classes of experience, there has been a total lack of cross-fertilisation between psychiatric and parapsychological research, each being apparently oblivious of the other.

Attempts to link depersonalisation experiences in the normal section of the population to any diagnostic category have uniformly failed. The only characteristic specific to those who report these experiences is (somewhat predictably) one of introversion (Reed and Sedman 1964, Sedman 1966). There have also been attempts to link the depersonalisation states in patients to some known diagnostic category. Other than a possible association with depression these too have had little success (Sedman 1970). Psychiatrist Martin Roth proposed the somewhat quixotic hypothesis of a 'phobic anxiety-depersonalisation syndrome', which roughly translated means that depersonalisation is an attempt to escape from anxiety and stress by abandoning the ego's normal relationship to the environment. Unfortunately, the occurrence of depersonalisation seems to show little or no relation to anxiety states. The only test which does seem to show a clear distinction between depersonalised and non-depersonalised patients is the Linten-Langs Questionnaire, originally designed to evaluate the degree to which a subject is in an ASC! (Sedman 1968).

It seems probable that these experiences are potentially normal. Again, what distinguishes the healthy experience from the pathological one is the reaction of the individual; depersonalisation experiences in patients are invariably un-pleasant and prolonged. Depersonalisation and OBES are probably quite consistent with what is experienced in other ASCS, pointing to the transient nature of the social self or ego from which consciousness expands in these states.

Possession states

The phenomenon of entering a trance and being possessed by a spirit is common to most cultures and comes to ours as the mediumship of spiritualism. It is often argued that mediumship can be equated with secondary personality, but as we noted in Chapter Three, there are important differences. Mediumship is often not a pathological splitting of personality but a means through auto-hypnosis of forming new personalities in response to the needs of the bereaved. The paranormal evidence suggests that it can also be a 'transpersonal state' in which there is a merging with other minds.

The shaman's possession state in many ways fulfils the same function as mediumship. He enters into trance communication with gods and spirits to develop visionary and prophetic powers. Claudio Naranjo has recently (1972) published a fascinating account of shamanism. While agreeing that it can be a psychotic-like state in which the individual is overwhelmed by the unconscious, he argues that we have too narrow and negative a view of the unconscious, which can also express the latent *supernormal* as well as the abnormal, and provide the growth points of personality. The possession states often take the form of a disease so that 'under the pretext of an alien spirit in his body, the patient may express himself, say what he wants, satisfy his personal needs'. Naranjo draws an interesting comparison of this with the techniques of psychodrama and encounter group therapy. Yet psychosis does overlap with possession and can occur if the person is unable to deal with the avalanche of repressed material (and there is probably also a parallel with psychedelic effects here).

An example of this occurs with automatic writing. Naranjo (1971) quotes two examples of possession states which result from this. One is the case of Ludwig Staudenmeier, a professor of chemistry who began automatic writing out of curiosity but 'once that Pandora's box of his mind was open, his life became a struggle to master the forces he had unleashed in his own psyche'. The other example is Emmanuel Swedenborg, the Swedish statesman and universal man of science. His dictations were at first biblical ramblings but later became the source of a high level of creativity. Both Staudenmeier and Swedenborg were said to possess paranormal abilities, particularly in connection with what we would now call psychokinetic phenomena. Again this seems to be confirmation of the unconscious as a 'gold mine as well as a rubbish heap'. We have already mentioned the case of the automatic writing of Patience Worth, suggesting that a great range of potential ability can be tapped in this way.

Psychokinesis—the apparent movement of objects by thought —finds its main representation in poltergeist phenomena. There is now quite a formidable amount of evidence in favour of the authenticity of some cases, but at one time poltergeist cases, as the name might suggest, were attributed directly to possession by evil spirits. Recent research by William Roll at the Foundation for Psychical Research and Hans Bender of the University of Freiburg lends support to the psychodynamic view, that they often appear to be an expression of repressed aggressive feelings stemming from one individual; usually, it is widely believed, an adolescent (Roll 1970, Bender 1969). Emotional linkages of some sort seem to provide the foundation for most paranormal phenomena.

Psychedelic states

Psychedelic drugs have made widely available experiences previously restricted to a few mystics and shamans. Although there are dangers in the illicit use of the drugs, the evidence (presented in the next chapter) strongly suggests that when they are used with adequate psychological preparation in a supportive setting, they can be a source of creative, therapeutic and even mystical experience.

Experiences during psychotherapy

Many individuals during hypnotic, meditative, psychedelic and occasionally psychotic states claim to have experienced a growth in personality towards a unification with inner selves and feelings of which they were previously unaware. Effective therapy may involve a similar change in experience to those reported by individuals in altered states.

Until recently, psychotherapy has been based largely on the

intellectual process of interpreting unconscious feelings and fantasies said to stem from infantile experiences. The last few years have seen a proliferation of therapies aimed at bringing together the total functioning—both intellectual and feeling —by methods as apparently diverse as meditation, primal therapy, encounter groups, and Reichian and Rogerian therapies. Of these, the existential or client-centred therapy of Carl Rogers has a substantial amount of empirical backing.

Rogers is sceptical of the relevance of professional qualification and intellectual or diagnostic knowledge to the effectiveness of therapy. Instead, he places emphasis on universal qualities; those of non-possessive warmth, empathy and genuineness (in not playing a role). He argues that psychological disturbance arises through love and acceptance being *conditional* during the formation of our identities. As a result we have had to distort and selectively perceive much of our potential experience in order to be loved and liked by others. The argument then goes that in order to reunite parts of the patient's experience, the therapist must be empathic, accepting and warm. Because the acceptance and positive regard or warmth of the therapist is unconditional—in that there is no fear of rejection—the patient can have a non-threatening perception of experiences which was previously denied (Rogers 1961). A large amount of evidence has in fact accumulated to show that these factors do promote greater self-exploration and experience of new feelings and meanings. This seems to be so much so that there is evidence that therapy can act in two directions, making the patient better or worse depending on the level of the therapist's empathy, warmth and so on (Truax and Carkhuff 1967). The same principles may also be employed in encounter groups to promote an accepting milieu in which social games are exposed and more authentic ways of relating explored. The end result has often been described as an expanded awareness.

Rather than attributing these changes to an unconscious, Rogerian therapists claim it is a matter of becoming aware of unformed feelings. Psychotherapist Eugene Gendlin (1961) prefers to describe therapy as increasing the use of experiencing by encouraging the subject to become aware of feelings which are present but not conceptualised. One of the great paradoxes of the unconscious was that it implied the existence of thoughts which were formulated below the threshold of consciousness. But this becomes redundant if we allow for the existence of potential experiences and feelings which can be reached by the widening of consciousness beyond the limits set by our usual concepts of self.

It is interesting that Rogers focuses on empathy and supportive factors as responsible for facilitating this growth, the same factors which have independently been found to be decisive influences in altered states and paranormal phenomena. Certainly, there are many examples of the occurrence of apparent telepathic experiences during therapy (Devereaux 1953) which would seem to confirm these links.

One contribution which seems to have come from research in the field of ASCs and ESP is the suggestion that there are higher planes to inner experience. Psychedelic states, creative states and automatisms provide tentative evidence for what have been called 'transpersonal experiences'. Knowledge gained from these seems to transcend the waking potential and it may be that the expanded consciousness can engage other minds. Existential psychologist Abraham Maslow has talked of 'peak experiences' as characteristic of self-realised individuals. By this he means that the ability to have mystical experiences may be part of the higher potential of the self. This is obviously the other end of the pathology-health dimension. But one thing seems definite: altered states provide an axis point for either disturbance *or* growth.

7
Psychedelic States

Probably more than any other single influence, the growth in the use of psychedelic drugs is responsible for the contemporary interest in inner experience and subjective reality. With it has come a torrent of controversy, claims and counter-claims varying from mystical union with God at one extreme to chromosomal damage at the other.

Although LSD is a relatively new drug (first synthesised by Hoffman in 1938), the experience is an old one. 'Natural' psychedelic drugs have been used to alter man's consciousness since the time of earliest records; the cannabis plant, for example, is listed in a Chinese compendium dating from 2737 B.C. The Aztecs appear to have used the equivalent of most modern psychedelic drugs; a type of morning glory seed containing LSD derivatives was used for inducing visions, sorcery and communicating with the gods. In their sacramental rites they used a sacred mushroom, 'teonanacatl' (which means flesh of the gods), and the Peyote cactus. The psychoactive ingredients of these plants are, respectively, psilocybin and mescaline. With the arrival of the Spanish conquistadores and their missionaries, all these drugs became the object of harsh suppression—the Spaniards were afraid of the divine and visionary powers associated with them, and attributed these to diabolic possession.

The witches of the sixteenth and seventeenth centuries used the plants datura, henbane and belladonna in their ointments, which may explain their visions of flying to the Sabbath and partaking in orgies with the devil. But psychedelics were not only used for demonic rites, datura was apparently employed by the oracle at Delphi for inducing possession by a god. It has also been suggested that the 'miracles' of the Jews may have been due to their unleavened bread containing the ergot fungus, another LSD derivative. The names of many plants—'flesh of the gods', 'sacred mushroom', 'vine of the souls'—all bear reference to the religious experiences associated with their use.

One cannot help seeing a parallel between the irrational fear of some earlier cultures and the irrational element in the present-day sanctions on psychedelic drugs. Despite the existence of contradictory research evidence, newspaper reports cultivate the impression that psychedelics have been responsible for addiction to hard drugs, chromosomal damage, suicide and psychosis. Considering that government consent is given mainly to research attempting to demonstrate harmful effects of marijuana and LSD, it is surprising how little evidence there is for the ill effects of these drugs when they are used in appropriate settings.

There is in fact little evidence that pure LSD produces any chromosomal damage (Dishotsky *et al.* 1971), and it is ironic that any chromosomal damage is probably due to the impurities in black market drugs. As we noted in the previous chapter, there are virtually no suicidal or psychotic reactions when the setting is supportive.

Sidney Cohen (1960) has summarised forty-four research studies, totalling 25,000 drug administrations to 5,000 persons. Among the volunteer subjects there were no suicides, addictions or evidence of harmful physical effects. Hallucinations lasting more than forty-eight hours occurred in only .08 per cent of cases, and of the psychiatric patients, 2 per cent had hallucinations lasting longer than forty-eight hours and 1 per cent attempted suicide (with .04 per cent succeeding).

A similar situation seems to have arisen with marijuana. In reality, most authorities agree that the arguments used against it are invalid (Grinspoon 1969). Particularly suspect are the medical studies which confuse many variables, and which Tart (1971) has justly satirised as 'reminiscent of the medical literature on masturbation in the last century'. Rather than relying on the results of groups of inexperienced users in a laboratory setting, Tart conducted a phenomenological survey into what had been experienced by those who had used the drug a dozen times or more. Inevitably, it was generalisation from a pro-marijuana college sample and therefore very biased, but the results were intriguing. At moderate levels of intoxication all the senses were reported to be stimulated, perception more organised and meaningful, time slowed and the here and now more important. Social relationships were reported to be improved and less 'game-like', with sexual relations more enjoyable.

There is in fact a hard core of evidence to support the suggestion that psychedelics have an unexploited creative, therapeutic and religious potential. Unfortunately, the curtailing of research by legal restrictions has meant that experimentation has gone little further than the exploratory stage. What research there is, however, suggests that psychedelics could open up whole new areas of psychology. It has been said that the study of LSD might provide for unification and a new orientation in psychology and parapsychology, in a similar way to what occurred in the biological sciences with discovery of DNA.

The Harvard controversy

One of the major episodes contributing to the prohibition of LSD was the unprecedented dismissal of Leary and Alpert from their posts at Harvard. Leary, a clinical psychologist of some repute, was known for his research on personality and psychotherapy. Following an experience with the sacred mushroom, his interest focused on the religio-mystical effects associated with psychedelic drugs.

By 1963 the team at Harvard included several creative and productive psychologists; Timothy Leary, Ralph Metzner, Richard Alpert and psychiatrist Walter Pahnke. Of the group, Leary was particularly articulate and persuasive. After publishing several studies with Alpert on the effects of psychedelic drugs, he began zealously to advocate their more general use, maintaining that the experience was too valuable to be monopolised by scientific and medical circles.

The result was that much of the pioneer work in this area was swallowed up in a wave of hysteria and the two sides have since become completely estranged. Perhaps this was inevitable, but it has also meant that, since 1966, very little further knowledge has been gained about psychedelic experiences. Indeed it is very difficult in the present climate to write about such experiences without risking an emotional reaction.

The nature of psychedelic experience

As with all ASCs, one can approach psychedelic effects in two ways; either by cataloguing behavioural changes and symptoms associated with the use of the drug concerned, which is essentially the medical approach (e.g. Cohen 1967, Glass and Bowers 1970), or by attempting to explore the experience of the individual concerned and its meaning to him, the phenomenological approach (e.g. Masters and Housten 1966, Tart 1971).

To catalogue behavioural changes and symptoms would be long and laborious; body image disturbances, changes in self percepts, enhancement of sensory perception, alterations in perception of space and time, hallucinations, paranoid delusions. . . . Instead, the phenomenological orientation—the one preferred here—attempts to get behind diagnostic words to an understanding of the subjective reality of the individual. It emphasises how the experience is one in which the normal concepts of space, time, logic and causality are relinquished, permitting the individual to explore his own 'inner space' of personal meanings in a dynamic and philosophical way. For example Leary, Metzner and Alpert (1964) state: 'A psychedelic experience is a journey to new realms of consciousness. The scope and content of the experience are limitless, but its characteristic features are the transcendence of verbal concepts, space-time dimensions and ego or identity.'

Because the content is so unlimited, it is difficult to describe a typical experience; but a main feature of the psychedelic state is its individuality. A case that illustrates not only the space-time transcendence but several other common aspects is an LSD experience described by a twenty-year-old psychology student. The drug had been taken in an uncontrolled, largely non-supportive environment.

I became aware of awareness itself, I became my inner core of experiencing and I felt intensively and uniquely alive. This was frightening at first, because it also involved the disintegration of my outer social self and seeing myself as a set of façades and games played to the world. But an escape was implied as well as anguish, since, in being liberated from the ego, consciousness was able to perceive its unity with the world. Initially, I felt only more anxiety, for this meant that even the security of such absolutes as logic, time and space was lost. When this was accepted, the novelty of this insight into nature made me almost ecstatic and I felt I had perceived a fundamental truth. Yet, in writing this account, I understand what is meant by the transcendental nature of the psychedelic experience, for the language I use is an imposition which cannot translate the immediacy and richness of the experiences, some of which were outside our normal concepts. One became enraptured with texture, colours and shapes, and with life itself, as though the world was being perceived for the first time. But there were fearful parts even here, for people were seen symbolically, according to their meaning to me, as demons, saintly figures, witches, elves, etc.

Later, I could understand the self-analytic level of the psychedelic state. I had been reading Jung and Hesse at the time and the experience became a journey through my unconscious, meeting parts of my self which had apparently been denied, and reliving forgotten childhood traumas. At times there was a solipsism in which I felt only I existed, and the world I perceived became dominated by these personal fears and fantasies. Obviously some of this was terrifying and I can see how the psychedelic experience can be dangerous if such fears are overwhelming and the person is unable to deal with them. On the other hand, I felt that the drug did not result in your becoming aware of anything that wasn't there (at least potentially) before, and therefore in the absolute sense you could be no worse off.

The above is a good example because it illustrates that the experience is not always positive and enhancing but can be horrific and delusory as well. The decisive factors are the expectations or 'set' of the individual, his personality and the setting.

The influence of set and setting

Of all the ASCS, the psychedelic state is probably the most sensitive to interpersonal influences, described previously as experimenter and subject expectancies, the 'demand characteristics' of the situation, and such factors as empathy and the relationship of those involved. Indeed, it has been argued that the drug merely acts as a catalyst for the release of potential experiences, and how these experiences are received depends entirely on intra- and inter-personal factors.

The interaction of setting with personality helps to explain the different and sometimes untoward experiences that occasionally result from taking psychedelics 'on the street' versus, say, the analyst's couch. In a supportive setting the individual may reach unresolved feelings and be able to work through them, while the unprepared use of LSD and other psychedelics can result in a superficial, purely sensory experience. Because it may also elicit unresolved fears and fantasies—particularly if these are strong and the circumstances unfavourable—it can also result in the personality being swamped by these in a psychotic type of experience.

Although I know of no study specifically designed to explore the effects of psychedelics given under supportive versus unfavourable conditions (such a study would, at the least, be unethical), Theodore Barber (1969) has extensively reviewed the evidence relevant to these influences. He considered as the three main variables drug dose, situation, and set, plus personality. Dosage, he concludes, does not seem related in any clear way to the major effects while, conversely, situation and set seem major determinants. Suggestions given implicitly and explicitly by the experimenter and his attitudes and expectancies all seem to affect the moods and emotional reactions of the psychedelic subject. Regarding the subject's own set and personality, Barber concludes that 'personality variables play an important role in determining both the overall intensity of the reaction to LSD and the degree to which the subject becomes anxious or paranoid during the LSD session'.

The effects of less potent psychedelic drugs such as marijuana may be equally amenable to the influence of set and expectancy. Barber has recently (1972) quoted a study in which marijuana users were 'confused' by being injected intravenously with alcohol or saline while they were smoking either a marijuana cigarette or a placebo cigarette without its cannabis ingredient. This resulted in the subjects being unable to distinguish whether they were becoming drunk or 'stoned'!

Such consideration of the setting in which the psychedelic drug is taken helps to reconcile many of the apparent contradictions in the research findings. This is especially true of the claims and counter-claims made for the effects of psychedelics on therapy and creativity as well as, as we shall see later, extrasensory perception.

With the qualification that virtually all studies suffer from lack of adequate control comparisons, reviews of the evidence (Mogar and Savage 1964, Mogar 1965) suggest that psychedelics can facilitate therapeutic improvement in a wide range of disorders. This is particularly true of diagnostic groups such as alcoholics, criminal recidivists, and autistic children who do not respond well to more orthodox forms of therapy. Certainly the success rate here is well above spontaneous remission rates.

Again, a supportive setting appears to be crucial to the efficacy of LSD therapy. In his own study, for example, which seemed to show extraordinary success, Roger Mogar assessed the effects of LSD on almost 400 subjects, paying specific attention to the situation and context of the experience. After a series of preparatory interviews, the LSD was administered in 'a comfortable, aesthetically pleasing setting' with emotional support available if it was required. All diagnostic sub-groups were reported to show positive personality changes over the two- and six-month follow-up periods and 'the nature and extent of improvement compared most favourably with longer-term, orthodox therapies'.

A means of further maximising the effect of expectancy in LSD therapy may be to combine it with hypnotic suggestion. Comparisons of combinations of LSD with hypnosis and therapy have shown the triple combination, or 'hypnodelic state' as it has been called, to be the most effective (Ludwig and Levine 1966). This use of hypnosis with LSD therapy may also be effective because it allows some control over the direction of the experience, mitigating any onslaught of fears and delusions.

The effects of setting and expectancy have been even more neglected in research on the creative potential of the drugs. The basis for this research is the claim that psychedelic drugs promote new associations and ways of seeing things as well as empathy with one's surroundings. There are many spontaneous reports, especially by artists, of improved creative output following the use of LSD,[1] but attempts to validate this in an experimental setting have met with little success; the methodology that was often employed might just as well have been used to test the performance of a new grade of petrol.

The standard practice was to give batteries of creativity tests to graduate students before and after the psychedelic experience, comparing any changes in score with a control group which received no drug. The flaw was the assumption that the psychedelic creative experience could occur in a vacuum and that tests would measure it. It overlooks the fact that subjects undergoing a psychedelic experience are unlikely to be interested in doing a battery of psychological tests. Moreover it is doubtful that graduate students have a high performance level on creativity tests.

Probably the only study to give adequate attention to the context in which the drugs were taken was conducted by Willis Harman and his colleagues (1966) at the Institute of Psychedelic Research at San Francisco State College. They worked with

[1] See R. E. L. Masters and J. Housten, *Psychedelic Art* (Grove Press, New York, 1968).

twenty-seven male subjects representing a wide range of careers, all of whom had come to solve some specific practical problem connected with their job. In pre-session interviews the subjects were given the expectancy that they would not become pre-occupied with personal problems but that the mescaline they were to be given would permit them to use new ways of perceiving their problems rather than those available by the usual cognitive processes. They were introduced to each other and encouraged to work as a group and separately. Following the mescaline experience there were significant changes on tests of creativity and favourable subjective reports, but most important was the finding that nearly all the problems which they had worked on without progress for several weeks or months, received a solution of 'pragmatic utility'. By this it was meant that attempted solutions were accepted, used or further worked on in their job.

In accounting for their success, Harman and his colleagues stressed the importance of sufficient support and preparation for the experience: 'It is essential to recognise the crucial importance of all persons involved in the session and of the psychosocial milieu in which the session is conducted. . . . The confidence of E (the experimenter), based on personal experience that the process "works", is an essential ingredient. The psychedelic subject is extremely sensitive in his heightened state of empathic awareness to doubt conveyed by E.'

Harman *et al.* went on to list ten dimensions of the psyche-
[...]ate relevant to its creative potential which can be
[...] in either a facilitative or inhibitory direction depending
[...] interaction of the experience with the situation. For
[...], in accordance with the orientation that the subject is
[...]ged to have, the experience can either move outwards
[...] empathic involvement with surroundings or inwards
[...] a preoccupation with personal problems.

[...] sensitivity of the psychedelic state to subtle influences
[...] bedevilled parapsychological research into it. Again, we
[...]umerous reports of spontaneous incidents of extra-
[...] perception associated with the use of psychedelic drugs

(e.g. Krippner 1968) but conflicting experimental findings. The final irony is that several researchers have themselves recorded the occurrence of ESP during a psychedelic state (Osmond 1961, Krippner 1967), but when the studies are looked at in terms of procedure, the familiar differential is revealed. Of the four studies in this area, only the one which produced some ostensible evidence of ESP concentrated on developing a situation conducive to the task, while the remaining three apparently did not.

ESP in the psychedelic state

Whether or not psychedelic drugs are objectively conducive to extrasensory perception, there seems little doubt that, following their use, individuals are more open minded to such phenomena. 76 per cent of a sample of marijuana users believe in ESP (Tart 1971), and 75 per cent of a sample of LSD users reported they were more open minded after taking the drug than before (Harman 1964).

One can explain this in different ways. It may be that the experience of 'other worlds', with their transcendence of normal space-time relations, breaks down our logical defences against such experiences as ESP. Indeed, this in turn may promote an increased frequency of ESP experiences associated with the drugs. Alternatively, the sceptic can use the same argument—that psychedelics break down 'ego boundaries' between the self and others, thereby promoting regressive, animistic beliefs. Only empirical research can decide which of the two views is correct.

In an excellent review of the difficulties involved in such research, the psychotherapist Duncan Blewett (1963) has suggested that the psychedelic experience must first be 'stabilised' before an attempt can be made to utilise it. Usually the state is not stable but rather a kaleidoscope of images and feelings which are being discovered and explored. The self dissociates from this and as 'ego loss' ensues objectivity is impossible, which can result in either self-acceptance or rejection, culminating in an experience anywhere between the psychotic and self-realisation ends of the dimension. Obviously such psychological problems and feelings must be worked through and resolved before experimentation can be tried. Another problem noted by Blewett is that the psychedelic experience is often a fusing of empathy and telepathy, but a non-verbal one for which research may need new methods, such as being able to identify the 'feeling style' of subjects.

Even this may be a generalisation from a psychotherapeutic context. As we shall see later, subjects will experience levels varying from the purely sensory to the mysical, depending on the situation and the support they receive. At a sensory level subjects may be too fascinated by novel perceptions to become involved in dull experimentation, while at mystical levels, ESPs may seem too mundane and obvious so that experimentation appears a waste of time!

It is a sad fact that three out of the four pilot studies seem to have been grounded by these problems. Karlis Osis, parapsychologist at the American Society for Psychical Research, reported a study (1961) in which he gave LSD to mediums and asked them to do 'object reading tests'—to give information about the owners of objects that were presented to them. Unfortunately only one medium showed any signs of being successful and the whole thing proved unsatisfactory because the mediums became too involved with and distracted by their own personal problems.

Another study, by biochemist Roberto Cavanna and psychoanalyst Emilo Servadio (1964), became virtually an exploration of methodological difficulties. LSD and psilocybin were used and strict screening was felt to be necessary to eliminate any risks to the subject, which left them with only three, two of whom were supposed to be controls for the one remaining sensitive. No preparatory adjustment or prior experience with the drugs was apparently given to help stabilise the experience. 'Improbable' qualitative materials were used as ESP targets; a picture of a foot, for example, combined with a wrist watch. A rating assessment of the degree of correspondence between responses and targets (which is open to personal bias) was employed instead of the usual blind matching of responses and targets, but no quantitative evidence of ESP was produced.

The latest and most extensive study reported was carried out by the Dutch researchers S. R. Van Asperen de Boer, P. R. Barkema and J. Kappers (1966). While this seems to have been conducted in a proficient and meticulous manner it appears to have been at the expense of almost total neglect of interpersonal factors.

Having first tried LSD, they gave it up as too disturbing to work with. Instead they administered psilocybin, which is less severe in its effects, to their thirty subjects and followed it by Zener card guessing tests (for ESP), object reading tests, and travelling clairvoyance tests. While there was a definite indication of ESP in the scores from the Zener card tests, this showed no significant difference from scores in the control sessions without the drug. The other tests also produced some evidence of ESP but the scores again were little different from those obtained without the drug, and their two best subjects had claimed previous paranormal ability. Unfortunately, assessments also used ratings of correspondences which are open to bias. Symbolic representation seemed to occur with the psilocybin as, for example, one subject in response to an object reading test said the owner of the object had the name of an animal, 'Wolf', when his name was Wolfson.

The lack of success is understandable when we note that the authors reported that more than half the subjects were distracted by their experiences and many were said to make 'psychotic remarks'. Probably the most interesting finding was that there were differences between the ESP scores associated with the various 'target persons', or intended agents, for the ESP experience. This also seemed to be true of the ESP scores associated with the three experimenters themselves, although no formal assessment could be made of either of these findings.

Besides the neglect of relationship and interpersonal factors, a major deficiency common to these three studies is the absence of preparatory experience with the psychedelic drug which would have helped to stabilise the experience. Apparently no previous experience was given in the Osis and Cavanna-Servadio investigations, and only two out of the thirty subjects in the Dutch series took the drug more than once.

But the remaining pilot study seems to have overcome many of these deficiencies. This was a study of telepathy during LSD sessions conducted by Robert Masters and Jean Housten at the Mind Research Foundation in New York. Masters and Housten were experienced in the use of psychedelic drugs, having spent about fifteen years in their research, and during this time they came across occasional instances of what looked like ESP, which they found sufficiently intriguing to inaugurate a pilot study.

One instance described by them involved an apparent travelling clairvoyance experience in which a subject reported seeing 'a ship caught in ice floes somewhere in northern seas', its name being given as the *France*. Two days later newspapers recorded that a ship named the *France* had been freed from ice near Greenland.

Masters and Housten's pilot investigation had two parts; an ESP card guessing series in which subjects attempted during their psychedelic experience to identify the cards the 'guide' was looking at, and an image test in which the 'guide' tried to imagine a scene described on a piece of paper and the subject also tried to experience it. Masters and Housten reported the results of the card guessing separately for high- and low-scoring subjects, twenty-three of whom averaged 3.5 hits over their ten runs each. This is far below what could be accounted for by chance, and since they describe these subjects as bored and poorly motivated, it may have well been a case of 'psi-missing'—where ESP is used to avoid giving the correct response. The remaining four subjects produced enormously high scores averaging a total of 8.5 hits for their ten runs each. These subjects were described as close friends of the guide, better motivated and with a high level of empathy.

Whether these scores are looked at separately or together, they could not arise by chance except statistically at less than once in ten million million times. The only alternative to ESP is to claim that non-verbal or subliminal forms of communication were responsible since the guide was often in the same room as the subject.

The image tests were unfortunately carried out under the same conditions, but these also produced an extraordinary high level of correspondence. Forty-eight of the sixty-two subjects 'approximated' to the guide's image on at least two occasions out of ten. The remaining fourteen were all persons not well known to the guide, and they experienced anxiety or were bored with the test. But on several occasions, subjects appeared to identify correctly what the guide was experiencing even when he was unable to imagine the target. Masters and Housten give a remarkable example of this in the following case.

	Paper in the envelope reads	*Guide imagines*	*Subject reports*
1	Viking ship tossed in storm	Same	Snake with arched head swimming in tossed seas
2	A rain forest in the Amazon	Same, with some exotic flowers growing	Lush vegetation, exotic flowers, startling greens, all seen through watery mist
3	Atlas holding up the world	Same	Hercules tossing a ball up and down in his hand
4	Greek island with small white houses built in terraced hills	Same but with an earthquake, houses falling down	A circus
5	A sail boat off a rocky coast	Same	Sail boat sailing around a cliff

Paper in the envelope reads	*Guide imagines*	*Subject reports*
6 Ski slope in New England white, with skiers sliding down	A forest fire. Guide was unable to imagine the ski scene	A forest fire
7 New York City traffic scene	Same but very brilliant colours	Geisha girl in full oriental regalia
8 A plantation in the old South	Many images relating to pre-Civil War plantation life, including a Negro picking cotton	A Negro picking cotton in a field
9 An arab on a camel passing a pyramid	Same	Camel passing through the inside of a vast labyrinthine tomb
10 The Himalayas— snow-capped peaks	Same	A climbing expedition in the Alps

Whether or not we accept the Masters and Housten study as providing evidence of ESP in the psychedelic state, it does illustrate the importance of the quality of the relationship— especially in terms of motivation and empathy—in this kind of research. Another distinctive feature of this study is that it used guides who had helped subjects through their psychedelic experiences, and therefore empathy was presumably high.

Because of the prohibition on psychedelics no further experimental research using LSD to induce ESP has been reported, so the only remaining approach is to observe it in subcultures where psychedelics are used illicitly. Stanley Krippner, psychologist in the Maimonides team, and anthropologist Don Fersh (1968, 1971) have made an innovative field study of ESP in hippie communes. They visited twenty-two communities in the south-western USA and noticed that 'one common element which permeated them was the report of paranormal experience'. Although Krippner and Fersh did not observe any of these events at that time, six members of one commune paid a visit to the Maimonides Dream Laboratory. They went into the laboratory sound room while an assistant chose a target to look at. The group consensus opinion was that it was 'a machine on which there were buttons'; the target was a typewriter. During the second attempt the assistant tried to send an image of a bridge and each member of the commune was questioned individually. This time two of the six said 'bridge' and a third said 'suspension bridge'.

This kind of research can possibly throw light on whether or not the frequent use of psychedelics in a free life style does promote an openness to ESP, but it seems doubtful whether much more can be learned about the nature of the relationship of the psychedelic experience to ESP without further controlled experimentation.

Another claim for psychedelic drugs is that with many subjects in a facilitative setting a genuine mystical experience will result. This is obviously a claim of enormous significance since, if it proved valid, it would mean that experiences previously limited to a few mystics could now become available for study. This would open the doors to unthought-of areas of psychology and religion and possibly provide a long-needed theoretical framework for parapsychology.

Can the psychedelic state produce a mystical experience?

The answer with certain reservations seems to be yes; with setting, expectancy and support as vital constituents of the experience.

There have been about five or six studies on this (Ditman *et al.* 1962, Janiger and McGlothlin 1963, Leary *et al.* 1963, Masters and Housten 1966) which suggest that if the setting is supportive, between 30 per cent and 55 per cent of psychedelic subjects will report a religious type of experience; if the setting is both supportive and religious the percentage is considerably higher, probably about 70 per cent. Well over half of these subjects described it as the most important experience in their life.

But is the effect a genuine religio-mystical experience or a counterfeit product of the drug and the situation? Leary (1970) has contended that since the psychedelic experience provides 'the ecstatic, incontrovertibly certain, subjective discovery of answers to seven basic spiritual questions' such as 'what is life?' or 'who am I?', it is by definition a religious-type experience.

The late Walter Pahnke, in his doctoral dissertation on the psychology of religious states, attempted to answer this question (Pahnke 1966, Pahnke and Richards 1966). Pahnke systematically compared the psychedelic state with mystical consciousness. Having derived nine criteria from the writings of mystics which seemed to provide a descriptive summary of their experiences, he showed that these could apply equally well to his subjects' psychedelic experiences. These criteria were feelings of unity with the universe and of perceiving the ultimate reality, transcendence of space and time, a sense of sacredness, positive feelings of love and benevolence, ineffability, and a feeling that the experience was transient but could at the same time produce lasting positive changes in personality.

It must be stressed, however, that Pahnke's subjects were theology students; it was Good Friday, the atmosphere was religious, and subjects and guides listened to a two-and-a-half-hour religious service which included organ music, solos, prayers and meditations. Nevertheless, despite these conditions, nine out of the ten who had received psilocybin and only one of the controls had what appeared to be a genuine religious experience. The experiments were carried out under triple blind conditions, so that neither the subjects, the guides nor the experimenters knew who had received the psilocybin and who had received the placebo. Consequently the experiences were not solely an artifact of expectation and the religious setting (although these were probably important).

Consistent with this are the findings of Masters and Housten who employed strict criteria before concluding whether or not a subject had had a religio-mystical experience. Virtually all (96 per cent) of their subjects reported seeing some kind of religious imagery such as angels, devils, mandala shapes and so on. Even so, Masters and Housten allowed that an experience was religious or mystical only if there was some definite evidence of a lasting positive move towards 'psychological growth' or 'integration' of personality. Only eleven out of their 206 subjects fulfilled this criterion.

The evidence then suggests that a potential for mystico-religious experience is implicit in the psychedelic state, but whether this is genuinely realised depends on the preparation and support the experience is given. As we have seen, a parallel relationship seems to hold with the potential for creativity, therapeutic growth and extrasensory perception. The problem remains to interpret the meaning of the psychedelic state. Several models have been used. A recent autobiographical account by John Lilly (1972) even had the somewhat quixotic choice of using programming and computer analogies. Leary, Metzner and Alpert proposed a mystical approach based on the Tibetan Book of the Dead. This is an ancient Buddhist manual describing experiences to be expected at death, and the transitions consciousness goes through before its next incarnation. They also found it to be an accurate description of experiences during the psychedelic state. (Symbolically, at least, subjects frequently describe their experiences in terms of death and rebirth.)

Their aim in using this model was to facilitate the deepening of the psychedelic experience by freeing it from 'the games which comprise personality, and positive-negative hallucinations which often accompany states of expanded awareness'. The 'games of personality' are equated with the Buddhist doctrine of karma and the psychedelic experience is described as passing through several 'Bardo' levels or stages. The first level is of ego loss or dissociation of the self. This is followed by the Chonyid-Bardo level composed of images derived from the karma of personality and allegedly also from past lives and the history of the race. The final level involves the choice of a new personality.

Whatever we may think of this it does have an *experiential* agreement with what has been described by other researchers such as Masters and Housten. Instead of using models, they used the phenomenological or existential orientation (1966).

The phenomenology of psychedelic experience

Masters and Housten's *The Varieties of Psychedelic Experience* (1966) was and probably still is the most important study in this area. It summarised the results of 206 experimental psychedelic sessions coupled with interviews of 214 psychotherapy patients, volunteer subjects and persons who had taken the drug on their own. It made valuable distinctions between prepared sessions with guides and those of casual users, and clearly distinguished psychedelic experiences from psychotic states. However, the most important contribution was the use of phenomenological analysis to delineate four levels of experiencing which formed a contextual basis into which all psychedelic experiences could be fitted. Most subjects, especially those without preparation or guides, only reach the first two levels.

At the sensory level, which involves the intensification of aesthetic awareness of objects, music, colours and so on, the experience could be deepened through dextrous use of the setting by the guide. For example, he might play Beethoven's Pastoral Symphony while slowly peeling an ear of corn as the crescendo is reached. It is probably this level which is of creative value.

The recollective-analytic level is the first stage of the journey inwards in which infantile past experiences are relived and self images analysed. The recollective-analytic level obviously pertains to the therapeutic use of psychedelics.

The symbolic level was reached by about 40 per cent of their subjects. Vivid eidetic images became the gateway for mythological, historical and legendary scenes. Often the myth chosen depicted some meaning and destiny in the individual's life.

Universal myths and symbols are used, such as those written about by Carl Jung; myths of secret quests, child heroes, cycles of nature, Prometheus and Faust.

The forest is often chosen as a stage because it retains the enchantment and magic of legends and fairy tales. Pageants of medieval scenes with castles, executioners, dragons, maidens, princes and talking animals are common. Masters and Housten compare the guide's role in this to Virgil, in Dante's *Divine Comedy*, leading Dante who has become lost in the forest, through a multitude of legends and scenes populated with gods and godlings of the medieval world, until he transcends. time and space to reach cosmological hierarchies. These experiences probably also relate to the contemporary popularity of such books as Tolkien's *Lord of the Rings* and Hesse's *Steppenwolf*, in which there are similar phantasmagoria of archetypal images and struggles.

The Integral level is the religio-mystical level, reached only by a few subjects. During this the subject 'experiences what he regards as a confrontation with the Ground of Being, God, Mysterium, Noumenon, Essence or Fundamental reality'. The result is a positive restructuring of the self which the subject may describe as a rebirth.

It is unknown whether extrasensory perception relates to any of these levels. Subjects often report that empathic feelings become so expansive they merge into telepathic ones which provide the basic bonding of the universe. On the other hand, Masters and Housten's symbolic level corresponds well to the second Bardo level (Leary, Alpert, Metzner) of hallucinatory imagery, and it is to this level that Buddhists attribute paranormal abilities. Moreover, as we noted in the previous chapter, possession states (in which ESP is often claimed) appear to have much in common with this stage, but this begets the wider question of the derivation of such hallucinatory experiences.

It is often erroneously said that ASCs reveal no new knowledge. Here we have the reverse problem—a problem we first came across in the case of Patience Worth (Chapter One)—of accounting for the source of knowledge. What organises the psychedelic drama? Is there knowledge outside the subject's normal range? Masters and Housten comment on this.

Whether one will attribute this rich 'reporting', with its impressive note of immediacy, to recall previously learned but long since forgotten, or to subjects with access to materials from some other source, will depend upon theoretical orientation. . . . We find drug subjects with little or no scientific training describing evolutionary processes in some detail, spelling out the scenery of microcosm and macrocosm in terms roughly equivalent to those used by the modern physicist. . . .

Despite their intimate acquaintance with the phenomena, Masters and Housten are still left indecisively hovering over its exact meaning. In the end they suggest an explanation in terms of forgotten memories derived from the mass media— students regurgitating their *Time* and *Newsweek* magazines during psychedelic trips!

Leary (1970) and Lilly (1972), at the other extreme, suggest that there is direct observation and awareness of cosmic, atomic and cellular processes during psychedelic experiences. Leary further speculates that DNA may encode the archetypal history of the person and species, accounting for evolutionary experiences. In short they support a view of a pantheistic universe, a view which at present has more in common with Eastern philosophy than with Western science.

These speculations and questions are likely to remain unanswered, and one cannot help agreeing with Tart (1972) that the outlook for further knowledge in this area is bleak. The last reported project on ESP and psychedelics is seven years old and, given the present climate and the additional handicap of academic prejudice against ESP, there is unlikely to be any further progress in the next seven either.

8
Meditation, Mysticism and Alpha States

Along with contemporary interest in the practice of meditation there has been a corresponding increase in knowledge of its physiology so that, through meditation, Eastern mysticism and Western science have formed an unlikely alliance. This is based on the claim that meditation can produce a state of almost complete relaxation, a contention which has received considerable support from physiological studies. As well as this, physiology has produced a simulation of some of the aspects of meditation in the alpha state, the subjective state accompanying a high quantity of alpha rhythm, measured by the EEG and achieved by voluntary alteration in concsiousness.

But the aim of meditation goes much beyond alpha or relaxation states; it strives to liberate consciousness from the constraints of physiological needs and logical control. Accordingly, the techniques of meditation can be classified by the way in which they attempt to alter consciousness. There are essentially two methods: those involving concentration and focus of thought onto an 'object' of meditation, thereby freeing other forms of experiencing; and those attempting to enforce freeing by relinquishing the demands of the body and the external world (Naranjo and Ornstein, 1972). Roughly, this distinction separates the two major traditions of Buddhism and Yoga, Buddhism belonging to the former and Yoga to the latter.

Meditation employs a variety of objects and symbols on which to focus. These include religious shapes (mandalas), repetitive sounds (mantras), postures (mudras) and breathing exercises. The Sufis use repetitive exercises which are ritualised into a sequence of movements and sounds. The Hindu and Buddhist Tantra systems and Chinese Taoism all focus on various areas of the body, since the body with its bilateral form symbolises the union of opposites and is regarded as a shrine for the soul. The common aim of concentrative meditation is to allow consciousness to become absorbed into the object and then expanded into spontaneous awareness.

Both Yogic and Zen methods use mantras and breathing exercises, but the emphasis is different. Yogis believe that by deprivation of the basic drives of hunger, food, sex, sleep and so on, consciousness can be liberated from its physiological restraints. Consequently they attempt to achieve control over the autonomic (involuntary) functions of the body and the nervous system, from which derive the Yogic claims of controlling such functions as heart beats and oxygen consumption. As a result, their use of breathing exercises and mantras is different; the Zen method will contemplate the process of breathing or recounting the mantra, the Yogic method will concentrate on control of the process. This is because the Zen emphasis is on the here and now, on being aware of awareness itself. The Zen attitude towards renunciation of the world is also different— more of a detachment than an actual renunciation whose aim is to develop the skill of being in the material world without belonging to it or being determined by it.

Some Zen and Yogic methods have analogues in Western psychology. Sensory deprivation (in which subjects are isolated from the major forms of sensation and stimulation), for example, produces a variety of changes in perception, body image and consciousness similar to meditation. The Gestalt psychology of Frederick Perls, like Zen, places emphasis on the meaning of the word 'Now'. Abraham Maslow's brand of existential psychology, in a parallel way to Zen, distinguishes between actions which are due to higher motives and those which are due to basic drives or desires. This is particularly evident in his distinction between love which stems from or is directed at respect for each other's being, and love which is merely a satisfaction of dependency needs. As we shall see later, there are also many experimental findings which suggest that meditation as a conceptual area may eventually integrate with the rest of psychology, and may also help to free it from its somewhat limited and rigid view of human potential. But before we turn to these experimental findings, it would be useful also to look at meditation as part of the wider perspective of Eastern philosophy and mysticism.

Eastern mysticism

Hindu philosophy, of which Yoga is an integral part, is the oldest philosophy deriving from Pre-Aryan times. Its doctrine of 'Brahmanism' holds that there is an ultimate reality or ground of being which pervades the Universe. (This appears to resemble what devotees of psychedelic drugs and other movements call White Light; it is pure thought and transcendent.) The philosophy also entails a belief in karma and reincarnation, in which one's state of happiness or misery is decided by the past actions and lives of the soul—in accordance with the principle that you reap what you sow. Thus the world is seen as an ensnarement by desires—karma, which has to be worked through in order to evolve to higher states. Consequently the emphasis in Yoga is on renunciation of the world and its demands.

Buddhism has a similar doctrine of karma and a life-death-rebirth cycle, but individuality is seen as illusory; the ego is a succession of images, and the organism a transitory aggregate of physical and psychical attributes. Only those aspects of the Self and the world which are free from causes and desires are real, and this is the state of nirvana at which meditation is directed. In Zen meditation, nirvana is a development of reflexive consciousness, an awareness of the process of consciousness itself.

Paranormal phenomena are encountered in both Zen and Hindu traditions. In Zen meditation, there is a level of consciousness at which visions of monsters and demons are perceived along with a paranormal knowledge of events collectively called mayko. But Buddhists ignore these occurrences which they consider incidental, until consciousness has evolved to a level where it can understand and use them wisely (Naranjo and Ornstein 1972). The Yogic tradition's systematic classification of paranormal knowledge is called Abhijna. Five forms of psi are distinguished which correspond to those defined by Western parapsychology. There are siddhis (psychokinetic and psychosomatic effects), divyacaksus (clairvoyance), divyasrotra (clairaudience), paracittajnana (telepathy) and finally purvanirvasanusmrti (reincarnation memories). One major difference is that extrasensory and sensory perception are regarded as the same process, the latter being a narrowed and limited aspect of the former; this accords with the pantheistic philosophy. Great importance is also attached to recall of past reincarnations since, if past lives can be understood, then the individual is liberated from the effects of their karma (Smith 1966).

While much of Eastern mysticism may be outside the pale of scientific investigation, it is interesting to note how it corresponds with some of the experiences elicited through the use of psychedelics. Many of Masters and Housten's subjects experienced a symbolic level at which visions of mythological gods and demons were seen, and a few even reached a level of mystical union with the universe. Why there should be this consistency in human experience remains unexplained, since it cannot in this case be dismissed as cultural conditioning or expectancy.

Most of the hard-core research has been done on the physiology of meditation and on related alpha states. As with other states of consciousness, extrasensory perception is frequently met during the change or expansion of consciousness. Indeed, we would expect such a state to facilitate ESP if it involves any of the direct awareness of, or merging with, reality that experienced practitioners claim. As we shall see, some of the findings are producing an extraordinary amount of agreement in view of the complexity of the phenomena.

The effects of meditation

Meditation appears to be a 'hypometabolic state', a state of bodily relaxation in which physiological activities (especially those of the sympathetic nervous system) are reduced. Mental activity also appears to be passive and attenuated, a state which is characterised by the abundance of alpha rhythm.

Particularly interesting is that EEG studies of Zen and Yogic monks suggest that their meditation states differ in ways that we would predict from knowledge of their respective philosophies. Indian psychologists in their study of Yogic meditation discovered that Yogis showed no brain response to (as monitored by the EEG), and denied subjective awareness of stimuli such as loud noises, touching a hot glass tube, and having a strong light shone at them. As well as this they were able to raise their threshold to pain so that they could keep a hand in water at 4°C. for long periods without apparent discomfort (Anand *et al.* 1961). Another study showed that some Yogis could slow their heart beats (Wenger *et al.* 1963). Evidently such feats are quite consistent with the world-denying philosophy of Yoga and its emphasis on annulling desire by bodily control.

In contrast, a study by Japanese psychiatrists showed that the brains of their Zen monks continued to respond to external stimulus (in this case, clicks) long after normal subjects would have 'habituated,' or come to ignore its presence (Kasamatsu and Hirai 1966). This may reflect the importance attributed by Zen monks to attaining a high level of reflexive awareness of the content of consciousness.

Most of the remaining research has been done on Transcendental Meditation, a form of Yogic mantra meditation introduced to the West by the Maharishi Mahesh Yogi which, because of its standardised form, is easily amenable to research. A project of major importance in giving meditation respectability was carried out by physiologist Robert Wallace and cardiologist Herbert Benson at the Boston City-Harvard Medical Unit and the University of California. Their results showed that meditation reduced blood flow, oxygen consumption, and blood lactate level while increasing skin resistance. This suggested an effect opposite to that of anxiety and allowed meditation a possible therapeutic potential. There has been further evidence that it may reduce susceptibility to stress by stabilising some of the functions of the autonomic nervous system (Orme-Johnson 1971). An attempt was made recently to evaluate its effects with relation to the personality of meditators. William Seeman, Sandford Nidich and Thomas Banta at the University of Cincinnati (1972) administered a test derived from the writings of Abraham Maslow on self realisation—the degree to which a person expresses his higher potential and motives. Meditators produced higher scores on this than non-meditators, at least for some of the dimensions of the test, but as no comparison was made with a group about to start meditation, we cannot tell whether the meditation may be held responsible or whether meditators just happen to be more spiritual beings anyway.

All these findings would lead us to expect meditation to be a psi-conducive state. Its relaxed, passive nature corresponds to subjective experiences described by ESP subjects (White 1964), while the alpha activity abundant during meditation has been shown experimentally to have some relation to ESP. But perhaps the most facilitative factor lies in the subjective experiences of merging with others and the world around reported during meditation. It was this sort of claim that led Karlis Osis and Edwin Bokert (1971) of the American Society for Psychical Research to investigate whether ESP occurs during the meditative state. In an extensive study over a two-year period using some quite sophisticated techniques of analysis, they were able to isolate three of the dimensions of meditation which could precipitate ESP—the presence of feelings of 'self transcendence and openness to experience' combined with the person's intensity of mood. But even so, they were forced to conclude that the meditative state is related to ESP in a complex and highly individual manner. Possibly because of this, many experimenters have instead worked with alpha states, the experimental analogue of meditation, in which the EEG provides an objective index of the subjective state. Although an increase in the amount of alpha activity is a definite feature of the meditative state, its presence is also a characteristic of many other ASCs, as we shall see later. Its significance probably lies in monitoring the movement of attention from the external world to that of subjective reality. As such it is still a very crude measurement, representing only the surface electrical activity of the brain, a minute proportion of the total. Furthermore, it is best understood as a probable effect of an on-going subjective state and not as a determinant of that state.

Biofeedback, alpha states and ESP

About the same time that interest in meditation was first being aroused, Joe Kamiya, a research psychologist at the Langley Porter Neuropsychiatric Unit in San Francisco, began experimenting on what were later to be called biofeedback techniques. He made the extraordinary discovery that subjects could increase their alpha activity by voluntary alteration of their subjective state. To enable them to know when they were succeeding and to maintain the state, the presence of a tone was used to feed back any increase in alpha. Since then, biofeedback has become a viable field of research on its own, its most important finding being, perhaps, to show the degree of control that could be attained by consciousness over physiological processes. Previously, the functions of the autonomic nervous systems such as heart beat, digestion and blood flow were thought to be beyond the reach of voluntary control, but some recent experiments by Neal Miller and Leo DiCara at Rockefeller University cast doubt upon this. It is well known that rats will work for electrical stimulation of the 'pleasure centres' of their brain, which is one of the most potent rewards known. Miller and DiCara's rats were required, instead of 'work', to alter various autonomic functions; their blood flow, kidney functioning, and the electrical activity of their brain. The experiments were successful even to the level of their being able to alter blood flow specifically in one ear; even rats then seem capable of the kind of control over bodily processes claimed by Yogis!

The use of biofeedback techniques has given a wider perspective to ESP research; if an ESP conducive state can be found, then subjects can be trained through feedback to alter their subjective awareness to it. This is where the alpha rhythm is important because it seems to accompany the relaxed, passive but internally alert state—which is the closest description we have at present to a psi-conducive state (White 1964). There is other evidence that it is the shift in state towards inner-directed experience which is facilitative of ESP. The two sets of findings can be reconciled easily and simply if we assume that such a relaxed, passive state is conducive to shifting attention to an internally directed experience.

The investment and interest in discovering the parameters of this psi-plus-alpha state can be judged by looking at eleven studies in this area reported during the last four years (Honorton 1969b, Morris and Cohen 1969, Stanford and Stanford 1969, Stanford and Lovin 1970, Honorton and Carbone 1971, Honorton, Davidson and Bindler 1971, Lewis and Schmeidler 1971, Stanford 1971, Morris *et al.* 1972, Stanford and Stevenson 1972, Rao and Feola 1972). But one of the difficulties in forming a coherent picture from all these findings is that two different measures of alpha activity were used. Rex Stanford and his co-workers used changes in the alpha frequency as their measure while other groups used mainly the percentage of time spent in alpha activity. Stanford's series of experiments suggested that a directional shift of the mean frequency of the alpha rhythm of subjects during testing related to their ESP scores. In the most recently reported study (Stanford and Stevenson 1972) Stanford used himself as the subject, employing meditation to reach a relaxed state. Measures of alpha were taken during the mind-clearing and image-development phases, which indicated that slower alpha activity related to high ESP scores on the tests, and a shift in the frequency of alpha towards slower activity accompanied the highest scores. Ultimately, it is probably the change in state that is crucial since the alpha activity was used here as an index of such a change occurring between the phases of meditation.

An experiment by Honorton, Davidson and Bindler (1971) attempted to relate the three sets of measures: alpha, state and ESP. Instead of relaxation or meditation, they used the biofeedback technique to generate alpha and then compared ESP scores during this period with a period in which alpha was suppressed by the same method. Subjects also rated their depth of consciousness during these periods by means of state reports. An interesting link between the three factors was discovered, indicating that those subjects with the highest state reports during the generation of alpha also produced the highest ESP effect. And there was another result; those who experienced the greatest subjective shift in their state of consciousness during alpha generation obtained significantly higher ESP scores than those reporting little subjective shift. Possibly the association of ESP with a highly subjective state is a product of the amount of shift in state required to reach it and not the state itself.

If these formulations are valid, we should expect them to extend to subjects who have been shown to have a high sensitivity to ESP. What happens if an EEG recording is made when a high order of ESP is in progress? Robert Morris and co-workers (1972) at the Psychical Research Foundation were fortunate enough to be able to make an EEG recording with a 'sensitive' —Lalsingh Harribance—during a period in which some extremely high scores were obtained (P 10^{-12}). These were the highest ESP scores ever obtained with EEG monitoring. Harribance was required to guess the sex of individuals whose photographs were being looked at in a separate room. During this his highest scores were associated, as might have been predicted, with a greater time spent in alpha and with a change towards a greater amount of alpha. Harribance described the accompanying subjective state as one of meditation in which he attempted to relax and clear extranervous thoughts from his mind. Such a description repeatedly occurs in some form, and suggests that some fairly comprehensive patterns are at last beginning to emerge. Yet even in alpha and meditative states the situation is made more complex by the same dependence, as in other ASCs, on interpersonal influences. Stanford stressed the important influence on the results of factors such as his mood. Morris and his co-workers noted the correlation of Harribance's involvement and motivation for the task with whether his scores were high or low.

The other major pattern to emerge—the association of ESP with a shift in the subjective state of consciousness—acquires some further confirmation from a study of sensory deprivation. During sensory deprivation, subjects isolated from most forms of stimulation often report bizarre body-image distortions, depersonalisation, minor hallucinations and an increase in the intensity of colour. The severity or pleasure of the experience also seems to depend on the experimenter and situational factors, to the extent that the presence of a panic button and the way the subject is greeted by the experimenter are important (Orne and Schiebe 1964).

Pleasurable sensory deprivation experiences seem to be another experimental analogue of meditation, since both share the same reduction of stimulation from the external world and shift of attention to internal reality. Consequently it seems reasonable to expect that such changes in consciousness might also precipitate extrasensory experiences. In a study of ESP during sensory deprivation, Charles Honorton and co-workers (1972) at the Maimonides Centre isolated subjects from visual and auditory stimuli and then suspended them in a rotatory cradle to eliminate kinaesthetic (muscular) sensations. During the isolation period subjects were required to estimate any change in their state of consciousness. Selected at random, the ESP target was an art print and, following isolation, the subjects were presented with a set of cards containing the target and asked to rank the correspondence of each card to the imagery which had occurred. The results confirmed the view that ESP can emerge during a change in consciousness: subjects with an overall high state report and a strong change in state during isolation produced the highest scores. These were significantly above chance while the others were at a level expected by chance.

To complete the link with meditative states, sensory deprivation is usually accompanied by a large quantity of slow alpha rhythm. Because of this, some authorities argue instead that it is a hypnogogic or drowsiness period, but alpha is a feature which accompanies many different states of consciousness. As well as sensory deprivation and meditation, it occurs in stage one dreaming, out-of-the-body experiences, some trance states (M. Thompson *et al.* 1937), depersonalisation (Davison 1964), daydreaming and fantasy states (Foulkes 1966). As we previously suggested its significance lies mainly in indicating a redirection of attention to inner experience and personal reality. So far then, some shape and meaning are beginning to emerge from these findings, but it remains to question the validity of the subjective experiences which accompany these phenomena.

Mystical consciousness
In effect, the presence of extrasensory perception is the only independent variable or objective measure by which we can test some of the claims of mysticism and meditation to involve a direct perception of reality. But can we go further than this, and is there any justification for the pantheistic beliefs associated with religio-mystical states?

Perhaps the most authoritative figure to give his attention to this problem was William James. In his Gifford lectures at Edinburgh at the turn of the century he produced a diverse collection of religious and mystical experiences which seemed to show a far greater similarity than might be expected, considering that his examples ranged from Christian ascetics to Buddhist monks. About the same time, the Canadian psychiatrist R. Bucke had collected a similar anthology and coined the phrase 'cosmic consciousness' to describe the mystical experience of unity with the universe that seemed to be a feature common to most of the accounts.

While such concepts may have more affinity with Eastern philosophies they are certainly not absent from the West. Kant theorised that the logic, time and causality used by our waking consciousness act to limit our knowledge of the real (noumenal) world underlying our sensations. We can never stand outside ourselves and reach beyond the senses or beyond the encoding by the nervous system of this world. Henri Bergson, the French philosopher, took this point further with his view of the brain as a limiting organ for perception; we can only see part of the universe because the brain filters our perception. Thus it is memory that holds these percepts together, gives us our reality and creates the 'box' in which we live.

In a fresh approach to this topic, Robert Ornstein noted various inferences from modern physiological psychology which support this view. Some experiments by researchers at the Massachusetts Institute of Technology on 'What the frog's eye tells the frog's brain' are particularly interesting (Lettvin, Maturana, McCulloch and Pitts, 1959). Electrodes were implanted in the optic nerve of a frog's eye to record its reaction to various objects. After presenting the frog with an array of objects and movement, it was concluded that it interpreted the world around in four ways, all of which were important for survival. One set of neural detectors, for example, responded specifically to a change in the pattern of light produced by small bug-shaped objects moving across the frog's field of vision; everything else was ignored, which indicated that frogs would starve to death despite a supply of dead but stationary bugs. This selection of sensory data is not limited to frogs; there are numerous examples of it in humans. We become used to noise levels and learn to have expectancies which influence and sometimes dictate what we see and hear. Perception is now regarded as a complex transaction between the brain, the sensory systems and incoming information, with the brain feeding back on the information it receives; and this selection occurs even more at higher levels of abstraction. Thus we form 'personal constructs', or ways of seeing people, to which we expect their behaviour to conform. All of these strategies seem aimed at giving us control and the ability to predict within our world.

Mystical consciousness is claimed to transcend this filtering and selection, thereby inducing an opening-up of awareness to new dimensions of experiencing. But does the study of these dimensions remain outside the territory of science? James thought not and proposed a science of mystical and religious states to be formed by extracting their common features. This area has now been claimed by 'transpersonal psychology' and some work has been done on James's proposal; we have already mentioned the research of Walter Pahnke on mystical states of consciousness associated with the use of psychedelics. Mystical experience invariably has dimensions of reality, unusual intensity of perception and unity with the universe as well as an ineffability of the experience. But, as psychiatrist Arthur Deikman (1966) has pointed out, this content says nothing about its origin, whether it be from God or the unconscious. While I am disinclined to support the theist alternative, I admit that the concept of the unconscious requires considerable modification to allow it to accommodate the meaning and origin of mystical experiences, and to prevent it becoming a refuge unit for the disposal of unknowns.

As for James, he candidly admitted that, all things considered, his own allegiance was towards a pluralistic universe, a polytheism in which there is a god in each of us of which our individual selves may be mutilated expressions. I find it hard to disagree with this view and can do no better than end with a quote from James himself on the subject:

It must always remain an open question whether mystical states may not possibly be superior points of view, windows through which the mind looks out upon a more extensive and inclusive world. (James 1901.)

9
Is there a Post-Mortem ASC?

Psychical research began by questioning whether or not the human personality can survive bodily death, an issue which has bedevilled it ever since. Any book on the subject must inevitably confront the problem in some form—and not without some trepidation. Before the parapsychologists, generations of philosophers and theologians tackled it with a consistent lack of success, but one contribution which may be made is to collate some of the modern findings on ASCs with the older, traditional evidence by comparing reports of 'trips' into other worlds by the living with reports given by the dead (or their impersonators) during their 'trips' into this world. If such a region has any even existential validity, there should be some definite agreement about its topography—although this could merely represent the shared fantasies of mankind. The fact that ASCs are often accompanied by ESP experiences militates against such a simple explanation.

Since most research on ASCs is only about ten years old, it is doubtful that such a collation has been done before on any scale. Moreover, significant research results continue to emerge and are especially valuable because they question the either/or phrasing of the issue as well as the meaning of personality itself. Ultimately, it may be that the problem is best resolved at an individual level, during our own ASCs—just as ESP seems more easily understood during meditation, psychedelic states and peak experiences. But before looking further, it may be useful to take stock of the older evidence for survival of personality after death, and the evidence weighing against it.

The traditional evidence for survival

The bulk of this consists of the nineteenth- and early twentieth-century studies of mediumship. We saw earlier (Chapter Three) how the mediums Mrs Leonard and Mrs Piper were exonerated from any suspicion of fraud, and how the ultimate choice was between a hypothesis of 'Super ESP', used to effect an impersonation of the deceased individual, and accepting the notion of the survival of some factor. By comparison, the survival hypothesis seems more valid—if not on the grounds of plausibility then on the implausibility of the ESP hypothesis. Several good examples of communications seem to excel anything that could be reasonably explained by ESP from the living. (See, for example, the Edgar Vandy case summarized by Broad, 1962.)

The most convincing evidence for survival is that provided by the cross correspondence cases discussed in Chapter Three, which typically consist of crossword puzzle-like clues sent through several mediums which, when put together, form a reference to an obscure Greek myth or poem. The nucleus of clues seems too definite to have occurred by chance, and since the total script was conjointly produced through several mediums, the question of the identity of the organising agency cannot be avoided. There is an intention behind the scripts, or, as remarked by the eminent psychologist Gardner Murphy: 'There appears to be a will to communicate. It appears to be autonomous, self-contained, completely and humanly purposive' (Murphy 1961). This intention also manifests itself in the explanation given by the 'Myers' of Mrs Fleming's scripts for the poor quality of communications sometimes produced by mediums:

The nearest simile I can find to express the difficulties of sending a message is that I appear to be standing behind a sheet of frosted glass—which blurs sight and deadens sound—dictating feebly to a reluctant and somewhat obtuse secretary. A feeling of terrible impotence burdens me.

It is impossible to know how much of what I send reaches you and how much you are able to set down. (Quoted in Saltmarsh 1938.)

Not all the evidence favouring the survival hypothesis is of early nineteenth-century vintage. More recently, the same implication of an organizing agency emerged from some experiments Karlis Osis (1966) conducted with mediums who were trying to communicate with a deceased biologist on behalf of his wife. In order to reduce the possibility that the mediums derived the necessary information by ESP from her, a series of persons formed links in a chain conveying the questions and answers. The mediums gave veridical information and cross correspondences emerged in the messages sent through different mediums.

A similar difficulty to that of explaining cross correspondences exists with 'drop in' communicators who appear at seances and are unknown to both the medium and the sitters. Only later enquiries and research can confirm the details which they give of their identity and life. If fraud is ruled out and the source of information is only remotely accessible and, ideally, if several sources must be pooled to give the information, then we are left with the same problem; supposing this information *is* derived by ESP, who or what instigates and organises it? A series of such cases have been reported by Alan Gauld of Nottingham University (1971) in which, of the thirty-seven 'drop in' communicators, ten had their credentials and identity confirmed. The communications were received through the automatic writing of a group of sitters using the ouija board.[1] There seemed no doubt that ESP was involved, since specific names, addresses and occupations in these ten cases were all later found to be correct. It seemed highly unlikely that the information could have been acquired in any other way, such as subliminal perception, since the group had no possible connection with the person and the details of the communicator's biography were only found in remote publications or known to a few people. Moreover, as Gauld pointed out, the source of information did not follow any particular sequence or pattern such as certain newspapers—extensive checks were made on this.

[1] Consisting of an upturned glass and a circle of letters. Hands are placed on the glass and its automatic movements spell out messages.

One of Gauld's best cases was that of Adolf Biedermann. The communicating entity correctly gave his full name (except for one wrong letter), his age at death, the year of his death, the name of the house where he had lived in London, that he had had connections with London University, and other details such as his philosophical views and that he had owned his own business. The messages also appeared to express a similar personality to that of Biedermann. If it was an impersonation by one of the sitters' unconscious then it would be necessary to combine, by use of ESP, information from at least four sources to achieve this. So, even if we discount survival, we are left with the same problem; what or who draws together all the information from obscure sources, selecting some and disregarding others? On the other hand, if we accept the survival hypothesis, it is all too obvious that unless communication channels are exceptionally bad, survival is incomplete—some communicators even have trouble in remembering important facts such as their names! As psychiatrist Donald West once remarked, the most one receives 'are odd pieces of personal information and sporadic flashes of speech and mannerism reminiscent of the deceased. This suggests not direct contact with a spirit but at most a vague and distant influence percolating through the medium's rambling discourse' (West 1962).

Conceivably one might try to wriggle out of this, as the 'Myers' entity did, above, by claiming that there is a lot of interference with messages by the medium's unconscious. But this still leaves the devastating evidence against survival unaccounted for.

The traditional evidence against survival

Most orthodox psychologists and physiologists have always taken the view that either the mind is an epiphenomenon of the brain—in the way that, say, light is a concomitant of a chemical reaction—or even that mind and brain are two aspects of one and the same thing. Only the 'third force' of humanists, existentialists and phenomenologists give awareness any priority in their accounts of the world. This situation resulted from the gross dependence of mind on body and brain—as well as the recent rise of computer analogies. Obviously, on this basis, belief in survival of mind after bodily death is committing a logical fallacy. But there are still further objections to survival which E. R. Dodds, who accepts ESP but favours the Super ESP hypothesis, raises. A theory of survival almost necessitates belief in the notion of existence before birth; otherwise, from whence derives the capacity for survival? Besides heredity and environment there appears to be no third factor stemming from pre-existence. As Dodds says, this would imply that the new-born infant must be a mature mind in an infant body, whereas it seems to be very much an infant mind in an infant body, whose fate follows the juvenescence and senescence of the body. As we shall see later, if the evidence for reincarnation is accredited then this argument will lose much if not all if its power.

While not pretending that I can resolve the head-on clash between parapsychology and physiology, there are a few points that seem relevant. First, I find it valuable to recall Kant's view that such insoluble problems may stem from the very nature of mind itself—that the supposed solution may transcend our fixed logical perspective. This, in fact, may be why ESP and the mind-body relationship seem more easily understood in altered states when logic-space-time relations are expanded or, as claimed by some, transcended. With regard to the 'Super ESP' hypothesis, the fallacy seems to lie in its attempts to explain one unknown by another. To be complete and convincing, a hypothesis which explains the evidence for survival must also give an understanding of ESP. This, I believe, is where ASCs come in, by providing such a conceptual framework.

The relationship between ASCs and ESP

In the previous chapters, we advanced evidence for a hypothesis directly linking interpersonal factors and the subjective state, implying that empathy and expectancy, for example, are important determinants of experience in altered states. There is also evidence to suggest that these are important determinants of ESP, so that the relationship is probably a triangular one in which all three are related. Specifically, ESP seems to emerge during a change in these subjective states; but why should this be so? One can only speculate, but it may be that empathy and emotional proximity facilitate an overlap in 'personal spaces'—spaces in which common associations and emotional experiences link individuals. This is close to the theory put forward by Gardner Murphy (1956) that individuals consist of interpersonal fields (using 'fields' in an analogous sense to the gravitational and magnetic fields of the physicist) which interact and merge with each other. Expectancy and suggestion probably encourage changes in subjective state, and ESP may then emerge during such changes when the 'self', searching for information, derives some of it from an overlapping field.

We have surveyed a panorama of a dozen or so different states of consciousness. Besides suggesting the great potential diversity and richness of human experience, what do they have in common and what is their meaning? I have attempted below to tabulate some of their main features:

Summary of the phenomenology of ASCs

State of Consciousness	Level of Perception	Level of the Self
Waking	Reality, in terms of logic-causality, space-time	Social self
Hypnosis	Alterations in the above determined by suggestion	Dependent on suggestion
Mediumship and Trance States	Logic, causality, etc. usually retained by the controlling self	Secondary personality or repressed self, sometimes plus an unknown ESP factor
Dreams	Symbolic fantasy	Repressed self
Lucid dreams and OBES	Symbolic fantasy, sometimes plus ESP	A 'inner self' perhaps transcendental

State of Consciousness	Level of Perception	Level of the Self
Pathological States	Reality relations usually partially retained, distorted by repressed self	Repressed self
Psychedelics	Sensory, analytic, symbolic, mystical levels	Varies from social, repressed, to transcendental according to perceptual level
Mysticism	Unity of perceiver and object	Transcendental self
Post Mortem	?	?

Evidently these divisions are artificial since there is a tremendous overlap and transition into each other. An OBE can develop into a mystical experience, a hypnotic state can become psychedelic, and a psychedelic experience can become mystical.

As for the interpretation of these experiences, in an important publication to which we have referred several times, Tart (1972b) recommended that there be 'state specific sciences'; that is, phenomenologies of each state in which data is collected and analysed with respect to that state. The overlap in the various perspectives can eventually be compared. Whilst such an analysis is rather premature at the present time, there are recurring features, one of which is the transpersonal or transcendental dimension common to many of the states, feelings of merging with a greater self, or even a mystical union. Other levels of the self which are also commonly perceived are the symbolic or analytic levels which are apparently expressions of unexplored areas with which Jung and Freud were concerned. Finally, one other recurring feature is particularly striking; that of secondary personalities or claimed previous incarnations. These occur throughout hypnosis, mediumship, automatic writing, possession states, psychedelic and meditative states. I am probably on very shaky ground here, but it would be my guess that the universality of these experiences calls for a deeper explanation than that of oedipal complexes.

Reincarnation

The sheer incredibility of reincarnation usually causes one to dismiss it out of hand as belonging to the realm of superstition. A few years ago this would have been my own reaction, so one must acknowledge the courage of Ian Stevenson who risked ridicule to introduce reincarnation to the scientific arena. Stevenson (1966) presented twenty cases of alleged reincarnation in which he had interviewed the purported reincarnated individual, and the prior and present families. As one might expect, most of the cases were from Asian countries, but there were also some from the West. Typically, they commenced with a child claiming identity with an individual now dead and often from a neighbouring village. In some cases, communication of the information necessary for confabulation was ruled out. This sort of thing usually occurs at the age of about two and a half years when the child rejects the name given to him by his parents and begins producing memories of a previous home, demanding that he be taken there. Sometimes precocious mannerisms and sexual interests are shown and claims made for unusual skills and birthmarks belonging to the previous personality. In the case of Imad Elawar the claims began at the age of about two years and memories produced focused somewhat precociously on a lover belonging to the previous incarnation. Stevenson was actually present at the reunion with some of the prior family, and of sixteen declarations about the previous identity, fourteen were correct. Twelve of these were of a highly personal nature including, for example, the last words he had spoken and details of the layout of his house and belongings, so that the information was unlikely to have been acquired through normal channels.

The conventional explanation for reincarnation is that it represents either a vicarious identity thrust on the child by the parents, or repressed memories which have split off from the main personality, in short, a secondary personality. Some experiments by Edwin Zolek (1962) (mentioned previously) showed that if hypnotised subjects are instructed to invent a personality, this can be shown by later psychoanalytic interview to derive from repressed and unfulfilled wishes. Yet this theory would seem inapplicable to Stevenson's cases since the child at such an early age has no identity from which to reject or dissociate its memories. Even on pure Freudian theory one could not conceive of this happening before the age of five or six years. Moreover, rather than bringing any conceivable benefit to a family, such cases more often than not are a source of disharmony; the child may not only reject its identity but also the family's caste and eating habits, even to the point of starvation. Although then the memories of the previous incarnation may be powerful at first, they usually subside in about seven years and integrate into the new personality, a process which Buddhists liken to the rings on a tree trunk.

As for a plausible explanation, even a theory which supposes that the information is derived by ESP fails to explain the child's choice of a particular person as a model. One argument for the reincarnation doctrine is the wide range of applicability it would find (Stevenson 1961). Besides being the missing factor for which Dodd was looking, it would explain both the phenomenon of the child prodigy whose skill seems to outstrip both endowment and environment, and *déjà vu* experiences where places are unaccountably familiar. These could both be explained as previous incarnation memories. Certain phobias with no apparent psychological cause in present life, and instances where fear should have been eliminated by further experience, could also be explained as resulting from death circumstances or other experiences of a previous personality.

On any account reincarnation is an extravagant hypothesis which the reader may find hard to contemplate; yet, surprisingly, men of the calibre of William James (1901) gave it their sympathy. The most recent authority to consider it favourably was Gardner Murphy (1973), a distinguished and reputable figure in both psychology and parapsychology. Murphy's speculations are bolder than most—and explain more than most. He revamps Whateley Carington's old associate theory of telepathy, which hypothesised that the mind was composed of 'psychons' or images which linked together to form a web or psychospace of associations. After death the web disintegrates over time, so any survival of memories or personality may only be for a limited period. An analysis of the cross correspondence cases shows that all the best ones tend to occur in the first seven years. So the detached remnants of the associative web may well become telepathically linked to a second emerging personality. The laws governing this are probably also associative in that the second personality will interlink with an emerging personality with which it already has affinity. Cases thus tend to come from neighbouring village, rather than distant countries. Murphy admits there are deficiencies even in this theory: the ego is remembered in a self-conscious form so that 'the initiative seems more likely to come from an active, integrating force than from a tangle of associations'.

Some of the difficulties have been resolved by Stevenson's supplement to Murphy's theory. He agrees that as a general rule a person tends to be reborn near the place he died, or at least to have been associated with the place of rebirth. But the theory neglects the likely emotional element in the associations evident in many cases of alleged reincarnation. When the previous personality died in youth, for example, his retrieved memories may centre upon a lover belonging to that life, and the majority of cases do in fact concern intense though often negative emotions. Stevenson estimates that between 50 per cent and 70 per cent of his subjects had died violently in their claimed previous incarnation. It is also possible that as well as some emotional factors, some habits and purposes may also persist, although their fate obviously depends on the new experiences.

This of course has a similarity with the Buddhist belief of karma where the 'unresolved cravings' of one life, after a variable period, strive for expression through rebirth so that the birth-death cycle repeats itself until karma is worked out. Now, if 'unresolved cravings' or motivation for survival are factors determining survival itself, then we would expect Myers, Gurney and Sidgwick to be among the leading contenders—which indeed they are.

While not wishing to give allegiance to one particular theory, the temporary and partial survival hypothesis seems to me the most workable one on the market, with the added advantage of having some compatibility with clues gleaned from ASCs as to what a post-mortem state might be like.

Travellers' tales and the geography of inner space
It must first be stressed that experiences of 'other worlds' and 'inner spaces' would be readily confined to some recondite anthology of tales but for their paranormal content and the fact that proof of them is sometimes available. This is not to say that such experiences are objectively valid but that they have their own existential validity, and that ESP is the bridge between inner and outer reality.

There are some patterns to this inner reality. We have noticed, for example, how altered states of awareness frequently involve a confrontation, or exploration of unresolved areas of personality together with new meanings of existence. (This is particularly evident in mystical trance states.) Could this correspond then to the descriptions of inner reality sent back through mediums by the 'deceased' Myers and Gurney (Chapter Three) and mystics such as Swedenborg, all of whom maintained that post-mortem consciousness is a unity of consciousness with the unconscious? Similar notions also form part of what are perhaps the two most cogent theories of survival, advanced by the distinguished philosophers, C. D. Broad from Cambridge 'and H. H. Price from Oxford. Broad (1962) supposes that survival consists of images organised as a dream world which may become temporarily united with the medium during trance. He conceives of the 'possibility of partial coalescence, partial reinforcement, interference, etc., between . . . components of several deceased human beings in conjunction perhaps with non-human psychic flotsam and jetsam which may exist around us'. But this partial survival may only be attained by a few since such a small minority give evidence of survival.

Price (1953) predicts a similar but slightly more appealing prospect. His too is a world of mental images but, because there is no longer a brain to filter what we call ESP, 'It would be the joint product of a group of telepathically interacting minds and public to all of them', and there may be many such 'worlds' capable of linking those with common associations. It would then be a dream world, but governed by the laws of Freudian psychology rather than physics. In fact it may become a nightmare as well as a wish-fulfilment world, depending on the reaction of a particular personality to the dissolution of the barrier between the conscious and unconscious.

Obviously the views of Murphy, Stevenson, Price and Broad have much in common with actual experiences reported during ASCS. But it must be stressed that any current arguments for survival are based mainly on the consistency of patterns in the clues, and the clues may be false. Some progress, however, has been made. Ten years ago the survival issue had almost gone out of fashion in parapsychology since it was impossible to produce a testable hypothesis. Now, with the advent of research on ASCS, we can at least make some empirical predictions and suggestions for future experimentation.

Recent research on ASCS suggests that ESP may not be perceptual but rather a sharing of experience which occurs most easily when individuals are in an altered state of awareness, linked by common associations and empathic feelings. (The term extrasensory perception may in this sense be a misnomer, since even clairvoyance can be understood as an associative response.) If this is true, it is directly relevant to the survival issue to know the limits of this overlap. One approach mentioned earlier is to study the amount of shared experience between individuals in the same ASC. For example, we could ask whether two individuals having out-of-the-body experiences would independently report the same subjective world and effects upon it.

It will certainly be interesting if we can discover answers to such questions, but the larger question of survival is perplexing; should this be insoluble? A tempting conclusion would be that part of the purpose of life is to come to terms with and understand the meaning of death.

Traditionally, the importance of parapsychology has rested largely on the survival issue. But I would also like to suggest that this kind of research is of specific importance to the living. If, as the evidence indicates, ESP is an integral part of inter-personal relationships and subjective states, then this goes a long way to restoring to our actions a sense of purpose and meaning; it suggests that on some occasions, at least, the 'blind' forces of our nature may not be so blind.

Glossary

Alpha feedback A technique for increasing the alpha wave production by feeding back to the subject changes in the quantity of alpha he achieves, through voluntary alterations in his subjective state of awareness.

Alpha rhythm A wave form produced by the brain and recorded by the EEG, occurring at a frequency of eight to fourteen cycles per second (cps). Often associated with internal imagery.

Alpha state The subjective state which accompanies a high quantity of alpha rhythm; it is difficult to describe but involves passivity and relaxation and yet some degree of alertness.

Altered state of consciousness (ASC) A state of awareness which is subjectively different from that involved in the normal orientation of consciousness to external reality. It may involve changes in the perception of space, time, causality and self identity.

Automatism An action carried out by an individual without the awareness of the normal waking consciousness. In *automatic writing* scripts or messages are produced which seem to have an origin other than that of the waking self. Often a ouija board, a planchette, or a glass with a circle of letters on which the hand is placed, may be used.

Control The personality which purports to act as an agency for the conveyance of messages from the dead to the medium, and sometimes takes *possession* of the medium's voice.

Clairvoyance The direct perception of objects or events by means which do not involve the normal sensory channels. A form of ESP.

Cross correspondence A communication through a medium which involves a cross reference to messages produced by another medium, each medium being apparently unaware of what the other had produced.

Depersonalisation A psychiatric and diagnostic term which can be used loosely or in a specific sense. Used loosely it refers to any disturbance of body image in which the normal relation of the self to the body is altered. Used specifically, it refers to feelings of unrealness or disorientation of the self.

EEG-EOG Technique The physiological recording of the electrical activity of the brain (electroencephalogram) and the eye movements (electro-oculograph) which accompany imaginal states such as dreaming.

Encounter group A term used to describe an eclectic method deriving in part from the psychotherapies of Carl Rogers, Wilhelm Reich and Frederick Perls. There are many variations and specific forms, but all aim at the realisation of unused potentials or repressed aspects of functioning of which the individual was previously unaware. Usually they attempt to create a warm, accepting milieu in which forms of communication other than the verbal one can be used, with the emphasis on feelings rather than logic alone.

Existential psychology A broad term related closely to *humanistic* and *phenomenological* psychology. Experiencing and consciousness are given priority and the subjective world of the individual is studied from the point of view of its meaning to him. Well-known contemporary proponents include Abraham Maslow, Carl Rogers, and Ronald Laing.

Extrasensory perception (ESP) The awareness of an external event by means other than the senses; its main divisions include telepathy, clairvoyance, and precognition.

Guide A person who helps another to interpret the meaning of his psychedelic experience and provides emotional support when needed.

High-scoring ESP subject A person in a parapsychological experiment who produces results in excess of what could be accounted for by the laws of chance, and whose scores are indicative of ESP.

Hypnogogic period Subjectively, the drowsiness period between waking and sleep during which hallucinations are often experienced.

Physiologically, it includes several stages characterised by an increase in the presence of alpha rhythm and the slowing of eye movements.

Lucid dream A dream in which the dreamer is aware that he is dreaming, and can sometimes influence the outcome of the dream.

Meditation A hypometabolic state of intense relaxation and, in such as the Yogic and Zen Buddhist systems, a technique of achieving what seems to be mystical union with the universe. Most techniques involve the reduction of external stimulation or the absorption of consciousness into it.

Multiple personality See secondary personality.

Non-REM period (NREM period) A period of sleep in which there are no eye movements and subjective experience is usually described as thought.

Ouija board See automatism.

Out-of-the-body experience (OBE or OOBE) An experience in which the individual perceives himself to be located in a separate place from, or outside, his body. Subjectively, it often takes the form of 'floating' above the body and looking down upon it.

Paranormal A synonym for *psi* or *psychic*, referring to events which cannot be explained by the normal laws of nature.

Parapsychology The scientific study of paranormal phenomena such as ESP.

Phenomenology The study of the way consciousness influences perception. See existential psychology.

Possession A state in which a person's body seems to be controlled by another entity or centre of consciousness.

Post-hypnotic suggestion A suggestion given during hypnosis but which will have its effect during the period following the termination of hypnosis.

Precognition A form of ESP in which there is an awareness of future events.

PSI A synonym for psychic.

Psychedelic state An ASC induced by psychedelic drugs which usually involves profound changes in perception and self awareness.

Psychical research The older name for parapsychology; now often used to denote the study of spontaneous psychic phenomena as opposed to the experimental.

Rapid eye movements (REMs) Eye movements which accompany visual imagery.

REM periods Periods of rapid eye movements which are accompanied by dreaming. There is controversy as to whether it is a psychological period during which biochemical changes occur, or a period in which dreams fulfil a psychological need. Hence they are called REM periods rather than the more committal, dream periods.

Reincarnation The belief and doctrine that there is rebirth of at least some aspect of personality in another body during some period following death.

Secondary personality An ancillary self which appears as dissociated or split from the main, waking self. Often occurs during trance states.

Sensitive A modern term for a person who claims to possess ESP abilities. He may or may not enter mediumistic trances.

Stage One dreams An alpha rhythm, REM period in which dreams are reported.

Subjective state A state of consciousness which is personally meaningful but which may differ from the common consensus reality.

Telepathy The ESP of another person's thoughts.

Trance An ASC with reduced bodily activity, used here as inclusive of hypnotic, mediumistic and possession states.

Travelling clairvoyance Clairvoyance usually linked to hypnosis, in which the subject reports 'travelling' to a distant place and observing events there.

Transpersonal state A mystical state during which there is a feeling of merging with others on a higher order of reality, or reaching a higher level of the self.

Reading List and References

The following are the main abbreviations used in the list of references.

Amer. Arch. Gen. Psychiat.	American Archives of General Psychiatry
Amer. J. Psychiat.	American Journal of Psychiatry
Amer. J. Psychother.	American Journal of Psychotherapy
Brit. J. Psychiat.	British Journal of Psychiatry
Brit. J. Psychol.	British Journal of Psychology
Bull. Brit. Psychol. Soc.	Bulletin of the British Psychological Society
Int. J. Clin. Exper. Hypnosis	International Journal of Clinical and Experimental Hypnosis
Int. J. Parapsychol.	International Journal of Parapsychology
J. Abnorm. Psychol.	Journal of Abnormal Psychology
J. Abnorm. & Soc. Psychol.	Journal of Abnormal and Social Psychology
J. ASPR	Journal of the American Society for Psychical Research
J. Consult. Psychol.	Journal of Consulting Psychology
J. Exper. Psychol.	Journal of Experimental Psychology
J. Human. Psychol.	Journal of Humanistic Psychology
J. Nerv. Ment. Dis.	Journal of Nervous and Mental Diseases
J. SPR	Journal of the Society for Psychical Research
J. Transpers. Psychol.	Journal of Transpersonal Psychology
Percept. Mot. Skills	Perceptual and Motor Skills

Proc. ASPR	Proceedings of the American Society for Psychical Research
Proc. Inst. Psychophys. Res.	Proceedings of the Institute for Psychophysical Research
Proc. Parapsychol. Assoc.	Proceedings of the Parapsychological Association
Psychol. Bull.	Psychological Bulletin
Psychol. Rep.	Psychological Reports
Sc. Amer.	Scientific American
Scand. J. Psychol.	Scandinavian Journal of Psychology

AARONSON, B. 'Hypnosis, depth perception and psychedelic experience'. A paper presented at the Society for the Scientific Study of Religion 1965. Reprinted in C. Tart (Ed.), *Altered States of Consciousness*. Anchor Books, New York 1972.

ANAND, B. 'Some aspects of electroencephalographic studies in Yogis'. Reprinted in C. Tart (Ed.), 1972 op. cit.

Ås, A. 'Non-hypnotic experiences related to hypnotisability in male and female college students'. *Scand. J. Psychol.* 1962 **3**, 112–21

ASSAILLY, A. 'Psychophysiological correlates of mediumistic faculties'. *Int. J. Parapsychol.* 1963 **5**, 357–74

AZAM and DUFAY. 'Observations on clairvoyance'. *Proc. SPR* 1889 Vol 6 (16)

BACKMAN, A. 'Experiments in clairvoyance'. *Proc. SPR* 1891 Vol 7 (19)

BANNISTER, D. 'The myth of physiological psychology'. *Bull. Brit. Psychol. Soc.* 1968 **21**, 229–32

BARBER, T. 'Physiological effects of "hypnosis"'. *Psychol. Bull.* 1961 **58**, 390–419

— 'Toward a theory of "hypnotic" behaviour: the hypnotically induced dream'. *J. Nerv. Ment. Dis.* 1962 **135**, 206–21

— 'Hypnotisability, suggestibility and personality: a critical review of the findings'. *Psychol. Rep.* 1964 **14**, 299–320

— *Hypnosis: a Scientific Approach*. Van Nostrand-Reinhold, New York 1969

— *LSD, marihuana, yoga and hypnosis*. Aldine, Chicago 1970

— Review of 'On being stoned: a psychological study of marihuana intoxication' by C. Tart. *J. ASPR* 1972 **66**, 415–18

BARBER, T. and CALVERLEY, D. 'Multi-dimensional analysis of "hypnotic" behaviour'. *J. Abnorm. Psychol.* 1967 **74**, 209–20

— 'Toward a theory of "hypnotic" behaviour: replication and extension of experiments by Barber and co-workers (1962–1965) and Hilgard and Tart (1966)'. *Int. J. Clin. & Exper. Hypnosis* 1968 **16**, 179–95

BARBER, T. and GLASS, L. 'Significant factors in hypnotic behaviour'. *J. Abnorm. & Soc. Psychol.* 1962 **64**, 222–8

BARKER, J. 'Premonitions of the Aberfan disaster'. *J. SPR* 1967 **44**, 169–80

BELOFF, J. *The Existence of Mind.* MacGibbon & Kee, London 1962

— 'Parapsychology as science'. *Int. J. Parapsychol.* 1967 **69**, 91–7

BELOFF, J. and MANDELBERG, I. 'An attempted validation of the "Ryzl" technique for training ESP subjects'. *J. SPR* 1966 **43**, 229–49

BELVEDERE, E. and FOULKES, D. 'Telepathy and dreams: a failure to replicate'. *Percept. Mot. Skills* 1971 **33**, 783–9

BENDER, H. 'New developments in poltergeist research'. *Proc. Parapsychol. Assoc.* 1969 **6**, 81–102

BERGER, R. 'Experimental modification of dream content by meaningful verbal stimuli'. *Brit. J. Psychiat.* 1963 **109**, 722–40

BERGER, R. and OSWALD, I. 'Eye movements during active and passive dreams'. *Science* 1962 **137**, 601

BESTERMAN, T. 'Report of an inquiry into precognitive dreams'. *Proc. SPR.* 1933 **41**, 186–204

BJÖRKHEM, J. *De Hypnotiska Halluciantionetna.* Lund. 1942.

— 'Hypnosis and personality changes'; chapter in *K. Lundmark,* (Ed.) M. Johnson, Goteberg 1961

BLEWETT, D. 'Psychedelic drugs in parapsychological research'. *Int. J. Parapsychol.* 1963 **5** (1), 43–70

BRADY, J. and ROSNER, B. 'Rapid eye movements in hypnotically induced dreams'. *J. Nerv. Ment. Dis.* 1966 **143**, 28–35

BROAD, C. D. *Lectures on Psychical Research.* Routledge & Kegan Paul, London 1962

BURT, C. 'The concept of consciousness'. *Brit. J. Psychol.* 1962 **53**

CARINGTON, W. 'The quantitative study of trance personalities, New Series 1'. *Proc. SPR* 1939 **45**, 223–51

CASIER, L. 'The improvement of clairvoyance scores by means of hypnotic suggestion'. *J. Parapsychol.* 1962 **26**, 77–87

CAVANNA, R. and SERVADIO, E. 'ESP experiments with LSD 25 and psilocybin'. *Parapsychol. Monogr.* 1964 **5**

COHEN, S. 'Lysergic acid diethylamide: side effects and complications'. *J. Nerv. Ment. Dis.* 1960 **130**, 30–40

— *Drugs of Hallucination.* Paladin, London 1967

COX, W. 'Precognition: an analysis II'. *J. ASPR* 1956 **50**, 99–109

DAVISON, K. 'Episodic depersonalisation: observations on seven patients'. *Br. J. Psychiat.* 1964 **110**, 505–13

DEIKMAN, A. 'Experimental meditation'. *J. Nerv. Ment. Dis.* 1966 **142**, 101–16. Reprinted in Tart 1972, op. cit.

DEMENT, W. and KLEITMAN, N. 'The relation of eye movements during sleep to dream activity: an objective method for the study of dreaming'. *J. Exper. Psychol.* 1957 **53**, 339–46

DEMENT, W. and WOLPERT, E. 'The relation of eye movements, bodily motility and external stimuli to dream content'. *J. Exper. Psychol.* 1958 **55**, 543–53

DEVEREAUX, G. *Psychoanalysis and the Occult.* New York 1953

DINGWALL, E. (Ed). *Abnormal hypnotic phenomena.* Vol 1. Barnes and Noble, New York 1968

DISHOTSKY, N. *et al.* 'LSD and genetic damage'. *Science* 1971 **172**, 431–40

DITMAN, K. *et al.* 'Nature and frequency of claims following LSD'. *J. Nerv. Ment. Dis.* 1962 **134**, 336–52

DODDS, E. 'Why I do not believe in survival'. *Proc. SPR* 1934 **42**, 147–72

EDMUNDS, S. and JOLLIFFE, D. 'A GESP experiment with four hypnotised subjects'. *J. SPR* 1965 **43**, 192–4

ERICKSON, M. 'A study of clinical and experimental findings on hypnotic deafness: I Clinical experimentation and findings'. *J. Gen. Psychol.* 1938 **19**, 127–50

EVANS, C. and OSBORNE, E. 'An experiment in the electroencephalography of mediumistic trance'. *J. SPR* 1952 **36**, 588–96

FOULKES, D. 'Dream reports from different stages of sleep'. *J. Abnorm. & Soc. Psychol.* 1962 **65**, 14–25

— 'Theories of dream formation and recent studies of sleep consciousness'. *Psychol. Bull.* 1964 **62**, 236–47

— *The Psychology of Sleep.* Scribner's Sons, New York 1966

FOULKES, D., BELVEDERE, E., MASTERS, R., HOUSTEN, J., KRIPPNER,

S., HONORTON, C. and ULLMAN, M. 'Long-distance "sensory bombardment" ESP in dreams: a failure to replicate'. *Percept. Mot. Skills* 1972 **35**, 731–4

FOULKES, D. and VOGEL, G. 'Mental activity at sleep onset'. *J. Abnorm. Psychol.* 1965 **70**, 231–43

FOX, O. *Astral Projection.* University Books, New York 1962

FREUD, S. *The Interpretation of Dreams.* Allen & Unwin, London 1954

FROMM, E. and SHOR, R. (Eds.). *Hypnosis: Research Developments and Perspectives.* Aldine-Atherton, Chicago 1972

GARRETT, E. *My Life as a Search for the meaning of Mediumship,* London 1938
— 'Roads to greater reality'. *Tomorrow* 1958 **6**, (4)

GAULD, A. 'A series of "drop in" communicators'. *Proc. SPR* 1971 **55**, 273–340

GENDLIN, E. 'Experiencing: a variable in the process of therapeutic change'. *Amer. J. Psychother.* 1961 **13**, 233–45

GHISLEN, B. (Ed.). *The Creative Process.* Mentor Books, University of California Press 1952

GILL, M. and BRENMAN, M. *Hypnosis and Related States.* International Universities Press, New York 1959

GLASS, G. and BOWERS, M. 'Chronic psychosis associated with long-term psychotomimetic drug abuse'. *Amer. Arch. Gen. Psychiat.* 1970 **23**, 97–130

GLICK, B. and KOGEN, J. 'Clairvoyance in hypnotised subjects: positive results'. *J. Parapsychol.* 1971 **35**, 331 (Abstract)

GLODUS, G. 'An appraisal of telepathic communication in dreams'. *Psychophysiol.* 1968 **4**, 365

GOLDNEY, K. 'An examination into physiological changes alleged to take place during the trance state'. *Proc. SPR* 1938 **154**, 43–68

GREEN, C. 'Out of the body experiences'. *Proc. Inst. Psychophysic. Res.* 1968 **2** Oxford (a).
— 'Lucid dreams'. *Proc. Inst. Psychophysic. Res.* 1968 **1** Oxford (b)

GRINSPOON, L. 'Marihuana'. *Sc. Amer.* 1969 **221** (6), 17–24

GURNEY, E. 'Peculiarities of certain post-hypnotic states'. *Proc. SPR* 1886 Vol 4 Pt 11

GURNEY, E., PODMORE, F. and MYERS, F. 'Phantasms of the 'living'. *SPR*, London 1886

HALL, C. *The Meaning of Dreams.* Dell, New York 1959
— 'Experimente zur telepathischen Beeinflussung von Träumen'. *Z. Parapsychol. Grenz geb. Psychol.* 1967 **10**, 18

HARMAN, W. 'Some aspects of the psychedelic drug controversy'. *J. Human. Psychol.* 1964 **3**, 93–107

HARMAN, W., MCKIM, R., MOGAR, R., FADIMAN, J. and STOLARIFF, M. 'Psychedelic agents in creative problem solving'. *Psychol. Rep.* 1966 **19**, 211–27

HART, H. *The Enigma of Survival*. London 1959

HEYWOOD, R. 'The Sixth Sense'. Pan Books, London 1966

HILGARD, E. *Hypnotic Susceptibility*. Harcourt, Brace & World, New York 1965

— 'Altered states of awareness'. *J. Nerv. Ment. Dis.* 1969 **149**, 69–79

HILGARD, E. and TART C. 'Responsiveness to suggestions following working and imagination instructions and following induction of hypnosis'. *J. Abnorm. Psychol.* 1966 **71**, 196–208

HOLT, R. 'Imagery: the return of the ostracised'. *Amer. Psychol.* 1964 **19**, 254–64

HONORTON, C. 'Relationship between EEG alpha activity and ESP card-guessing performance'. *J. ASPR* 1969 **63**, 365–374

— 'Significant factors in hypnotically-induced clairvoyant dreams'. *J. ASPR* 1972 **66**, 86–102 (a)

— 'Reported frequency of dream recall and ESP'. *J. ASPR* 1972 **66**, 369 (b)

— 'Experimenter effects and ESP'. Paper presented at the 15th Parapsychol. Association Confer. Edinburgh 1972 (c)

— 'ESP and altered states of consciousness'. *Current Directions in Parapsychology*, Ed. J. Beloff 1973

HONORTON, C. and CARBONE, M. 'A preliminary study of feedback-augmented EEG alpha activity and ESP card-guessing performance'. *J. ASPR* 1971 **65**, 66

HONORTON, C. and KRIPPNER, S. 'Hypnosis and ESP performance: a review of the experimental literature'. *J. ASPR* 1969 **63**, 214–52

HONORTON, C., DAVIDSON, G. and BINDLER, P. 'Feedback-augmented EEG alpha, shifts in subjective state, and ESP card-guessing performance'. *J. ASPR* 1971 **65** 3, 308–24

HONORTON, C., DRUCKER, S. and HERMON, H. 'Shifts in subjective state and GESP: a preliminary study of ESP under conditions of partial sensory deprivation'. Paper presented at 15th Parapsychol. Association Confer. Edinburgh 1972

HONORTON, C. and STUMP, J. 'A preliminary study of hypnotically-induced clairvoyant dreams'. *J. ASPR* 1969 **63**, 175–84

JAMES, W. Gifford Lectures, Edinburgh 1901. *The Varieties of Religious Experience*. Reprinted Fontana, London 1960

JANIGER and MCGLOTHIN. Quoted in Masters and Housten, *The Varieties of Psychedelic Experience*. Holt, Rinehart & Winston, New York 1966, p. 254

JOUVET, M. 'Neurophysiology of states of sleep'. *Physiol. Rev.* 1967 **47**, 117–77 (a)

— 'The sleeping brain'. *Science J.* 1967 (b)

KAMIYA, J. 'Behavioural, subjective, and physiological aspects of drowsiness and sleep'. *Functions of Varied Experience*. Ed. D. Fiske and S. Maddi. Dorsey Press 1961

KASAMATSU, A. and HIRAI, T. 'An electroencephalographic study on the Zen meditation'. Reprinted in *Altered States of Conciousness*. Ed. C. Tart. Anchor Books, New York 1972

KEELING, K. 'Telepathic transmission in hypnotic dreams: an exploratory study'. *J. Parapsychol.* 1971 **35**, 330–1

KELLY, E. F. and KANTHAMANI, B. K. 'A subject's efforts towards voluntary control'. *J. Parapsychol.* 1972 **36**, 185–97

KRIPPNER, S. Quoted in 'The cycle in deaths among U.S. Presidents elected at 20-year intervals'. *Int. J. Parapsychol.* 1967 9 (3) p. 152

— 'The psychedelic state, the hypnotic trance, and the creative act'. Chapter in *Altered States of Consciousness*. Ed. C. Tart op. cit.

— 'Experimentally-induced telepathic effects in hypnosis and non-hypnosis groups'. *J. ASPR* 1968 **62**

KRIPPNER, S. and FERSH, D. 'Psi in hippie communes'. Proc. Int. Confer. on hypnosis, drugs, dreams and psi (1967). Eds. R. Cavanna and M. Ullman. Parapsychol. Found., New York 1968

— 'Psychic happenings in hippie communes'. *Psychic.* 1971 Oct.

KRIPPNER, S., HONORTON, C. and ULLMAN, M. 'A second precognitive dream study with Malcolm Bessant'. *J. ASPR* 1972 **66**, 269–79 (a)

— 'A long-distance ESP dream study with the "Grateful Dead"'. *J. Amer. Soc. Psychosom. Dent. Med.* 1972 **19**, (in press) (b)

— 'A precognitive dream study with a single subject'. *J. ASPR* 1971 **65**, 192–203

KRIPPNER, S., HONORTON, C., ULLMAN, M., MASTERS, R. and HOUSTEN, J. 'A long-distance "sensory bombardment" study of ESP in dreams'. *J. ASPR* 1971 **65**, 468–75

KRIPPNER, S. and ULLMAN, M. 'Telepathy and dreams: a controlled experiment with EEG-EOG monitoring'. *J. Nerv. Ment. Dis.* 1970 **151**, 394–403

LAING, R. *The Politics of Experience and the Birds of Paradise.* Penguin, London 1967

LEARY, T. *et al.* 'The religious experience: its production and interpretation'. *Psychedelic Review* 1964 **1**, 325

LEARY, T. *The Politics of Ecstasy.* Paladin, London 1970

LEARY, T., METZNER, R. and ALPERT, R. *The Psychedelic Experience: a manual based on the Tibetan Book of the Dead.* University Books, New York 1964

LETTVIN, J., MATURANA, H., MCCULLOCH, W. and PITTS, W. 'What the frog's eye tells the frog's brain'. *Proc. Inst. Radio Engineers* 1959 **47**, 1940–51

LEVINE, J. and LUDWIG, A. 'The hypnodelic treatment technique'. *Int. J. Clin. Exper. Hypnosis* 1966 **14**, 207–15

LEVY, WALTER J., DAVIS, JAMES W. and MAYO, ALLEN L. 'An improved method in precognition test with birds'. *J. Parapsychol.* 1973 **37** (2) 83–96

LEVY, WALTER J., TERRY, JAMES C. and DAVIS, JAMES W. 'A precognition test with hamsters'. *J. Parapsychol.* 1973 **37** (2), 97–104

LEWIS, L. and SCHMEIDLER, G. 'Alpha relations with nonintentional and purposeful ESP after feedback'. *J. ASPR* 1971 **63**, 455–67

LIFTON, R. Quoted in *Time* magazine Jan. 15th 1973

LILLY, J. 'Inner space and parapsychology'. *Proc. Parapsychol. Assoc.* 1969 **6**, 71–9

— *The Centre of the Cyclone.* Paladin, London 1973

LUTHE, W. 'Autogenic training: method, research and application in medicine'. *Amer. J. Psychother.* 1963 **17**, 174–95. Reprinted in *Altered States of Consciousness.* Ed. C. Tart. Anchor Books, New York 1972

MCCREERY, C. 'Psychical Phenomena and the Physical World'. *Proc. Inst. Psychophysic. Res.* 1973 **4**, London

MASLOW, A. *Motivation and Personality.* Harper & Row, New York 1954

MASTERS, R. and HOUSTEN, J. *The Varieties of Psychedelic Experience.* Holt, Rinehart & Winston, New York 1966

MITCHELL, E. 'An ESP test from Apollo 14'. *J. Parapsychol.* 1971 **35**, 89–107

MITCHELL, J. 'Out-of-the-body experience'. *Psychic.* 1973 March 44–7

MOGAR, R. 'Current status and future trends in psychedelic (LSD) research'. *J. Human Psychol.* 1965 **2**, 147–66. Reprinted in Tart 1972 (a) op. cit.

MOGAR, R. and SAVAGE, C. 'Personality changes associated with psychedelic therapy'. *Psychother.* 1964 **1**, 154–6

MONROE, L. *et al.* 'Discriminability of REM and NREM reports'. *J. Person. & Soc. Psychol.* 1965 **2**, 456–60

MONROE, R. *Journeys Out of the Body.* Doubleday & Co., New York 1971

MORRIS, R. and COHEN, D. 'A preliminary experiment on the relationships among ESP, alpha rhythm and calling pattern'. *J. Parapsychol.* 1969 33, 341 (Abstract)

MORRIS, R. L., ROLL, W. G., KLEIN, J. and WHEELER, G. 'EEG patterns and ESP results in forced choice experiments with Lalsingh Harribance'. *J. ASPR* 1972 **66** (2) 253

MULDOON, S. and CARRINGTON, H. *The Projection of the Astral Body.* Rider & Co., London 1956

MURPHY, G. *Three Papers on the Survival Problem.* New York 1952
— *Challenge of psychical research: a primer of parapsychology.* Harper & Brothers, New York 1961
— 'Research in creativeness: what can it tell us about extrasensory perception?' *J. ASPR* 1966 **60**, 8–21 (a)
— 'A Caringtonian approach to Ian Stevenson's twenty cases suggestive of reincarnation'. *J. ASPR* 1973 **67**, 117–29

MURPHY, G. and KLEMME, H. 'Unfinished business'. *J. ASPR* 1966 **60**, 306–20 (b)

MUSSO, R. and GRANERO, M. 'An ESP drawing experiment with a high-scoring subject'. *J. Parapsychol.* 1973 **37** (1) 13–36

MYERS, F. 'On telepathic hypnotism and its relation to other forms of hypnotic suggestion'. *Proc. SPR* 1886 Vol 4 Pt. 10
— *Human Personality and its Survival of Bodily Death.* Longmans, Green & Co., London 1903

NARANJO, C. and ORNSTEIN, R. *On the Psychology of Meditation.* Viking, New York 1971

ORME-JOHNSON, D. 'Autonomic stability and transcendental meditation'. *J. Psychosomat. Med.* (in press)

ORNE, M. 'The nature of hypnosis: artifact and essence'. *J. Abnorm. Soc. Psychol.* 1959 **58**, 277–99.
— 'On the social psychology of the psychological experiment: with particular reference to demand characteristics and their implications'. *Amer. Psychol.* 1962 **17**, 776–83

ORNSTEIN, R. *The Nature of Human Consciousness.* W. H. Freeman, San Francisco 1972

OSIS, K. 'A pharmacological approach to parapsychological experimentation'. Proc. Two Confer. on Parapsychol. & Psychopharmacol. Ed. E. Garrett, Colonial Press 1961

— 'Linkage experiments with mediums'. *J. ASPR* 1966 **60**, 91–124

— 'Toward a methodology for experiments on out of the body experiences'. *Research in Parapsychology*. Ed. W. G. Roll, R. L. Morris and J. D. Morris 1972

OSIS, K. and BOKERT, E. 'ESP and changed states of consciousness induced by meditation'. *J. ASPR* 1971 **65**, 17–65

OSIS, K. and CARLSON, M. 'The ESP channel—open or closed?' *J. ASPR* 1972 **66** (3), 310–19

OSIS, K. and NESTER, M. 'Deathbed observations by doctors and nurses'. *Int. J. Parapsychol.* 1962 **4**, 27–56

OSMOND, H. 'Variables in the LSD setting'. Proc. Two Confer. on Parapsychol. & Pharmacol. Parapsychol. Found., New York 1961

PAHNKE, W. 'Drugs and mysticism'. Int. J. Parapsychol. 1966 **8**, 295–320

PAHNKE, W. and RICHARDS, W. 'Implications of LSD and experimental mysticism'. *J. Religion & Health* 1966 **5**, 175–208. Reprinted in *Altered States of Consciousness*. Ed. C. Tart, Anchor Books, New York 1972

PALMER, J. 'Scoring in ESP tests as a function of belief in ESP. Pt 1 The Sheep-Goat Effect'. *J. ASPR.* 1971 **65**, 373–408

PARKER, A. 'Some success at screening for ESP subjects'. *J. SPR.* 1974

— 'Precognition in gerbils using positive reinforcement'. *J. Parapsychol.* 1974

PARKER, A. and BELOFF, J. 'Hypnotically-induced clairvoyant dreams: a partial replication and attempted confirmation'. *J. ASPR* 1970 **64**, 432–42

PODMORE, F. *Modern Spiritualism*. London 1902

PODMORE, F. and GURNEY, E. 'Third report of the committee on Mesmerism'. *Proc. SPR* 1884 Vol 2 Pt 5

PRATT, G. *On the Evaluation of Verbal Material in Parapsychology*. Parapsychological Foundation Monograph 1969

— 'A decade of research with a selected ESP subject: an overview and re-appraisal of the work with Pavel Stepanek'. *Proc. ASPR* 1973, Vol 30

PRATT, G. and PRICE, M. 'The experimenter-subject relationship in tests for ESP'. *J. Parapsychol.* 1938 **2**, 84–94

PRATT, G. and RANSOM, C. 'Extrasensory perception or extra-ordinary sensory perception? A recent series of experiments with Pavel Stepanek'. *J. ASPR* 1972 **66**, 63–85

PRICE, H. H. 'Survival and the idea of another world'. *Proc. SPR* 1953 **50** (182), 1–25

PRINCE, M. *The Dissociation of a Personality.* New York 1961

PRINCE, W. F. *The Case of Patience Worth.* Boston Society for Psychic Research 1927 (reprinted by University Books 1964)

RAO, R. K. *Experimental Parapsychology.* Charles C. Thomas, Springfield, Illinois 1966

— 'A change of methodology is needed'. *Research in Parapyschol.* 1972. Ed. W. G. Roll, R. L. Morris, J. D. Morris

RAO, K. and FEOLA, J. 'Alpha rhythm and ESP in a free response situation'. *Research in Parapsychology* op. cit.

RECHTSCHAFFEN, A. 'Sleep and dream states: an experimental design'. *Psi Favourable States of Consciousness.* Ed. R. Cavanna, Parapsychol. Found., New York 1970

RECHTSCHAFFEN, A., VOGEL, G. and SHAIKUN, G. 'Interrelatedness of mental activity during sleep'. *Arch. Gen. Psychiat.* 1963 **9**, 536–47

REED and SEDMAN. 'Personality and depersonalisation under sensory deprivation conditions'. *Percept. Mot. Skills* 1964 **18**, 659–60

RHINE, J. B. Chapter in *Experimental Hypnosis*, Ed. L. Le Cron, Macmillan, New York 1952.

— 'Special motivation in some exceptional ESP performances'. *J. Parapsychol.* 1964 **28**, 41–50

RHINE, L. 'Precognition and intervention'. *J. Parapsychol.* 1955 **19**, 1–34

— 'Psychological Processes in ESP experiences, Part I waking experiences; Part II dreams'. *J. Parapsychol.* 1962 **26**, 88–111, 172–99

RICE, G. and TOWNSEND, T. 'Agent percipient relationship and GESP performance'. *J. Parapsychol.* 1962 **26**, 211–17

RICHET, G. 'Further experiments in hypnotic lucidity or clairvoyance'. *Proc. SPR* 1889 Vol 6, Pt 15

ROBERTS, W. 'Normal and abnormal depersonalisation'. *J. Mental Science* 1960 **106**, 478–93

ROGERS, C. *On Becoming a Person.* University of Wisconsin Press 1961

ROLL, W. 'Poltergeist phenomena and interpersonal relations'. *J. ASPR* 1970 **64**, 66–99

— 'Free verbal response and identikit tests with a medium'. *J. ASPR* 1971 **65**, 185

ROLL, W. and BURDICK, D. 'Statistical models for the assessment of verbal and other ESP responses'. *J. ASPR* 1969 **63**, 287

ROSENTHAL, R. *Experimenter Effects in Behavioural Research.* Meredith, New York 1966

targets'. *J. Parapsychol.* 1963 **27**, 227–41

RYCROFT, C. Chapter in *Psychoanalysis Observed.* Ed. C. Rycroft, London 1966

RYZL, M. and PRATT, G. 'The focusing of ESP upon particular

SALTMARSH, H. *Evidence of Personal Survival from the Cross Correspondences.* Bell & Sons, London 1938

SCHONBAR, R. 'Some manifest characteristics of recallers and non-recallers of dreams'. *J. Consult. Psychol.* 1959 **23**, 414–18

SEDMAN, G. 'Depersonalisation in a group of normal subjects'. *Brit. J. Psychiat.* 1966 **112**, 907–12

— 'An investigation of states of affect and alteration in consciousness as factors in the actiology of depersonalisation'. Unpublished PhD. thesis, University of Sheffield 1968.

— 'Theories of depersonalisation: a re-appraisal'. *Brit. J. Psychiat.* 1970 **117**, 1–14

SEEMAN, W., NIDICH, S. and BANTA, T. 'Influences of transcendental meditation on a measure of self-actualisation'. *J. Consult. Psychol.* 1972 May, 184–7

SHOR, R. 'Three dimensions of hypnotic depth'. *Int. J. Clinical & Exper. Hypnosis* 1962 **10**, 23–38. Reprinted in C. Tart (Ed.) *Altered States of Consciousness.* Anchor Books 1972

SHOR, R., ORNE, M. and O'CONNELL, D. 'Validation of a scale of self-reported personal experiences which predicts hypnotisability'. *J. of Psychol.* 1962 **53**, 55–75

SIDGWICK, E. 'On Evidence for clairvoyance'. *Proc. SPR* 1891 Vol 7 Pt 18

— 'A contribution to the study of Mrs Piper's trance phenomena'. *Proc. SPR* 1915 Vol 28

SMITH, H. 'Parapsychology in the Indian tradition'. *Int. J. Parapsychol.* 1966 **8**, 248–63

SPANOS, N., HAM, M. and BARBER, T. 'Suggested hypnotic visual hallucinations: experimental and phenomenological data'. *J. Abnorm. Psychol.* 1973 **81**, 96

STANFORD, R. 'Extrasensory effects upon memory'. *J. ASPR* 1970 **64**, 161–86

— 'EEG alpha activity and ESP performance: a replicative study'. *J. ASPR* 1971 **65**, 144–54
— 'Extrasensory effects upon associative processes in a directed free response task'. *J. ASPR* 1973 **67** (2), 147–90
STANFORD, R. and LOVIN, C. 'EEG alpha activity and ESP per-performance'. *J. ASPR* 1970 **64**, 375–84
STANFORD, R. and STANFORD, B. 'Shifts in EEG alpha rhythm as related to calling patterns in ESP run score variance'. *J. Parapsychol.* 1969 **33**, 39–47
STANFORD, R. and STEVENSON, I. 'EEG correlates of free response GESP in an individual subject'. *J. ASPR* 1972 **66**, 357
STEPHENSON, C. J. 'Cambridge ESP-hypnosis experiments (1958–64)'. *J. SPR* 1965 **43**, 77–91
STEVENSON, I. 'A review and analysis of paranormal experiences connected with the sinking of the *Titanic*'. *J. ASPR* 1960 **54** 153–71
— *The Evidence for Survival from Claimed Memories of Former Incarnations.* Surrey, England 1961
— 'Twenty cases suggestive of reincarnation'. *Proc. ASPR* 1966 **26**
— 'Precognition of disasters'. *J. ASPR* 1970 **64**, 187–210
— 'Carington's psychon theory as applied to cases of the reincarnation type: a reply to Gardner Murphy'. *J. ASPR* 1973 **67**, 130–45
STEWART, K. *Dream Theory in Malaya* 1966. Reprinted in C. Tart (Ed.) 1972 op. cit.
STUART, C. 'GESP experiments with the free response method'. *J. Parapsychol.* 1946 **10**, 21–35
SUTCLIFFE, J., PERRY, C. and SHEEMAN, P. 'Relation of some aspects of imagery and fantasy to hypnotic susceptibility'. *J. Abnorm. Psychol.* 1970 **2**, 279–87

TART, C. 'Frequency of dream recall and some personality measures'. *J. Consult. Psychol.* 1962 **26**, 467–70
— 'A comparison of dreams occurring in hypnosis and sleep'. *Int. J. Clin. Exp. Hypnosis* 1964 **7**, 163–70
— 'The hypnotic dream: methodological considerations and a review of the literature'. *Psychol. Bull.* 1965 **63**, 87–99 (a)
— 'Toward the experimental control of dreaming: a review of the literature'. *Psychol. Bull.* 1965 **64**, 81–92 (b)
— 'Types of hypnotic dreams and their relation to hypnotic depth'. *J. Abnorm. Psychol.* 1966 **71**, 377–82

— 'A second psychophysiological study of out of the body experience in a gifted subject'. *Int. J. Parapsychol.* 1967 **9**, 251–8

— 'A psychophysiological study of out of the body experiences in a selected subject'. *J. ASPR* 1968 **62**, 3–27

— 'Psychedelic experiences associated with a novel hypnotic procedure, mutual hypnosis (1968)'. Reprinted in Tart (Ed.) 1972 op. cit.

— 'Did I really fly? Some methodological notes on the investigation of altered states of consciousness and psi phenomena'. *Psi States of Consciousness*, ed. R. Cavanna, Parapsychol. Found., New York 1970

— *On Being Stoned: a Psychological Study of Marihuana Intoxication.* Science and Behavior Books, Palo Alto, California 1971

— (Ed.) *Altered States of Consciousness.* Anchor Books, New York 1972 (a)

— 'States of consciousness and state-specific sciences'. *Science* 1972 **176**, 1203 (b)

— 'Measuring the depth of an altered state of consciousness with particular reference to self-report scales of hypnotic depth'. In Fromm, E. and Shor, R. (Eds.) op. cit. 1972 (c)

TART, C. and DICK, L. 'Conscious control of dreaming: I The post hypnotic dream'. *J. Abnorm. Psychol.* 1970 **76**, 304–15

TART, C. and HILGARD, E. 'Responsiveness to suggestions under "hypnosis" and "waking-imagination" conditions: a methodological observation'. *Int. J. Clin. Exper. Hypnosis* 1966 **14**, 247–56

TAYLOR, W. and MARTIN, M. 'Multiple personality'. *J. Abnorm. & Soc. Psychol.* 1944 **39**, 281

THIGPEN, C. and CLECKLEY, H. *The Three Faces of Eve.* Secker & Warburg, London 1957

THOMAS, D. 'A proxy experiment of significant success'. *Proc. SPR* 1939 **45**, 257–306

THOMPSON, M. *et al.* 'Brain potential rhythms in a case showing self-induced apparent trance states'. *Amer. J. Psychiat.* 1937 **93**, 1313–14

THOMPSON, R. *Foundations of Physiological Psychology.* Harper & Row, New York 1967

TIMMONS, B. and KAMIYA, J. 'The psychology and physiology of meditation and related phenomena: a bibliography'. *J. Transpers. Psychol.* 1970 **1**, 41–59

TRUAX, C. and CARKHUFF, R. *Towards effective counseling and psychotherapy.* Chicago 1967

TYRRELL, G. *Apparitions*. Duckworth & Co., London 1953

ULLMAN, M. and KRIPPNER, S. 'A laboratory approach to the nocturnal dimension of paranormal experience: report of a confirmatory study using the REM monitoring technique'. *Bio. Psychiatry* 1969 **1**, 259–70

VAN ASPEREN DE BOER, S. R., BARKEMA, P. and KAPPERS, J. 'Is it possible to induce ESP with psilocybin? An exploratory investigation'. *Int. J. Neuropsychiatry* 1966 **5**, 447

VOGEL, A., FOULKES, D. and TROSMAN, H. 'Ego functions and dreaming during sleep onset'. *Arch. Gen. Psychiat.* 1966 **14**. Reprinted in Tart op. cit.

WALLACE, R. and BENSON, H. 'The physiology of meditation'. *Sc. Amer.* 1972 Feb. 84–90

WARR, P. 'Towards a more human psychology'. *Bull. Brit. Psychol. Soc.* 1973 **26**, 1–8

WATSON, L. and GUTHRIE, D. 'A new approach to psychopathology: the influence of cultural meanings on altered states of consciousness'. *J. for the Study of Consciousness* 1972 **5**, (1)

WELLS, B. *Psychedelic Drugs*. Penguin Books 1973

WENGER, M. *et al.* 'Voluntary heart and pulse control by Yoga methods'. *Int. J. Parapsychol.* 1963 **5** (1), 25–42

WEST, D. *Psychical Research Today*. Pelican Books, London 1962

WEST, D. and FISK, G. 'A dual ESP experiment with clock cards'. *J. SPR* 1953 **37**, 185–97

WHITE, R. 'A comparison of old and new methods of response to targets in ESP experiments.' *J. ASPR* 1964 **58**, 21–56

ZOLEK, E. '"Reincarnation" phenomena in hypnotic states'. *Int. J. Parapsychol.* 1962 **4** (3), 66–78

Indexes

Author Index

Subject Index